Calvin

Theologian and Reformer

Calvin
Theologian and Reformer

by
Joel R. Beeke
and
Garry J. Williams

REFORMATION HERITAGE BOOKS
Grand Rapids, Michigan

Calvin, Theologian and Reformer
© 2010 by Joel R. Beeke and Garry J. Williams

Published by
Reformation Heritage Books
2965 Leonard St., NE
Grand Rapids, MI 49525
616-977-0889 / Fax 616-285-3246
e-mail: orders@heritagebooks.org
website: www.heritagebooks.org

Library of Congress Cataloging-in-Publication Data

Calvin : theologian and reformer / edited by Joel R. Beeke and Garry J. Williams.
p. cm.
Includes bibliographical references.
ISBN 978-1-60178-091-1 (pbk. : alk. paper) 1. Calvin, Jean, 1509-1564. I. Beeke, Joel R., 1952- II. Williams, Garry J.
BX9418.C378 2010
230'.42092—dc22
2010014671

For additional Reformed literature, both new and used, request a free book list from Reformation Heritage Books at the above address.

Contents

Introduction

In 2009, five hundred years after John Calvin's birth, the John Owen Centre at London Theological Seminary held a conference to commemorate the life and work of the great Reformer. Calvin was born on July 10, so we were a little late when we gathered September 14 and 15 for the conference. Nonetheless, the event proved worth the wait. Afterward, a number of us felt that the papers presented at the conference were of sufficient quality and usefulness to merit wider dissemination. This volume contains the papers that were presented at the conference, albeit expanded and tidied up, but preserving something of the feel of live addresses intended primarily for the refreshment of pastors.

A few introductory words may help the reader to follow the rationale behind this particular selection of papers. The chapters are grouped into three sections: aspects of Calvin's life and work; his teaching on doctrine and experience; and his teachings on the Christian life and ministry. The book begins with Sinclair Ferguson's account of the life of Calvin. If you have not read Calvin's story before, you will find Ferguson's introduction accessible and thorough in covering the key details. If you know the story already, you will find this introduction a helpful reminder of its main elements. Towards the end of the chapter, Ferguson cites important lessons from the reformation of Geneva, finding it rooted in prayer and the Word.

The theme of Calvin the Reformer is explored in the second chapter by Ian Hamilton. Hamilton shows us how Calvin was subdued by God. This theme of the remarkable way Calvin was mastered by

Christ to spend his life serving Jesus Christ kept emerging during the conference. This self sacrifice is expressed in Calvin's personal emblem: a heart offered by hand to God. Calvin's example challenges us to lay down all of our time and energy in serving Christ. This chapter also draws attention to the ways Calvin's reforming work was motivated by a series of concerns. These concerns speak directly to the circumstances of our own times: his emphasis on worship to our worship wars; his insistence on doctrine to our doctrinal indifferentism; his longing for the peace of the church to the volleys of Reformed friendly fire; his passion for theological education to our pragmatic preference for the immediately practical; and his commitment to the Great Commission to our evangelistic timidity.

Tony Lane next introduces us to the *Institutes of the Christian Religion*. He describes the background of these editions, their English translations, their purpose, structure, and nature. He then entices us with some examples of Calvin's teaching, including some surprising and puzzling details. This chapter whets the appetite for more Calvin, in this case for more of his work in the *Institutes*. While wanting us to read the *Institutes* itself, Lane emphasizes Calvin's engagement with Scripture in a way that reminds us that Calvin was first and foremost concerned with the exposition of the Bible. The *Institutes* was intended to complement his commentaries and to serve the exposition of Scripture in the church.

With Calvin's writing in view, Paul Wells then provides the first of two essays on Calvin's doctrine, examining his teaching on union with Christ. Wells sets the wider context of this doctrine, explaining how the Incarnation of the Mediator bridges the gulf between the Creator and the creature, between God and man. He then looks at two fruits of the Incarnation. The first is the union of man to God that results from the Incarnation. The second is the distinction but not separation of justification and sanctification as the fruits of that union. Wells then explains three of Calvin's metaphors for union with Christ, exploring them from Calvin's comments on three biblical passages: engrafting from John 15:1–11, participation from Romans 6:1–11, and adoption from Romans 8:13–17. From this evidence, Wells concludes that union with Christ is the heart of Calvin's understanding of the gospel.

He leaves us with a richer understanding of what that means and how it functions within Calvin's theology.

Sinclair Ferguson writes the next chapter, exploring Calvin's teaching on the Holy Spirit. He shows how a particular doctrine can be pervasive in a theology without it having its own marked section or heading. It is especially striking to see how central the theology of the Holy Spirit was in Calvin's rejection of Roman Catholic theology. If we are to avoid propelling people who are hungry for the Holy Spirit into charismatic excess as the only place where He appears to be found, then it is vital that we emulate Calvin in his emphasis.

Calvin was supremely concerned about living out the gospel, so it is fitting that the book ends with two chapters concerning Christian life and ministry. Both of these are written by Joel Beeke, who served as my co-editor of this volume. In his first chapter, Beeke, together with the aid of Ray Pennings, proposes Calvin's emphasis on *pietas* as an alternative to the standard taxonomy of views on the role of Christians in society. Beeke and Pennings remind us of the broad outlines of the taxonomy before exploring the details of Calvin's teaching on piety. They show how Calvin was coherently religious and political, and provide a stimulating example of how debates that have been fixed in patterns can benefit from being considered in new perspectives. Calvin, writing long before modern classifications emerged, shows us how to maintain the importance of Christian engagement in a way that addresses criticisms that are levelled by those who favor a more separated approach.

For all his promotion of pious living, Calvin longed most to see the world reached with the Word. His theological works such as the *Institutes* were intended for preachers. Beeke's second chapter on Calvin the preacher is thus especially fitting to end the book. While the chapter includes some humbling facts about the extent of Calvin's preaching ministry, it also excites us with a refreshing vision of the power of preaching, according to Calvin. Preachers will find real encouragement here to persevere in their own ministry of the Word.

It was a pleasure to gather with two hundred other men at the John Owen Centre conference. The speakers came from the United Kingdom, France, and the United States, and there were delegates from all over the world. We experienced some of the unity that we have as Christ's people, as well as the mutual encouragement for which we have been given one another. Our prayer is that some of the blessing that we experienced at the conference will be felt by readers of these papers, and that we will be left saying with John Calvin, *Cor meum tibi offero Domine prompte et sincere* ("My heart, O Lord, I offer to Thee, promptly and sincerely").

— Garry J. Williams
Director, The John Owen Centre
for Theological Study, London

I. Life and Work

CHAPTER 1

Calvin the Man: A Heart Aflame

SINCLAIR B. FERGUSON

John Calvin ranks as one of the most significant figures in the history of the Christian church. Unlike his older contemporary Martin Luther or the later John Wesley, he did not "found" a denominational tradition as such, yet his impact on history in general and the history of the church in particular has been incalculable. From his influence on French literature to his contribution to democracy, he has been hailed as a pioneer. He bequeathed to later generations a small library of written material, but more than that, he exhibited an approach to Scripture, the gospel, and the life of the Christian that has inspired both scholarship and martyrdom. He was scholar, pastor, social and ecclesiastical reformer, political influencer, preacher, letter writer, theologian, and faithful friend.

Calvin is increasingly well served by the number of biographical studies in print.[1] In this brief chapter, I can touch on only a small

1. Among the more recent are: Alexander Ganoczy, *The Young Calvin* (1966), trans. David Foxgrover and Wade Provo (Philadelphia: The Westminster Press, 1987); T. H. L. Parker, *John Calvin: A Biography* (London: Darton, Longman and Todd, 1975); William J. Bouwsma, *John Calvin: A Sixteenth Century Portrait* (New York: Oxford University Press, 1988); Alistair E. McGrath, *A Life of John Calvin* (Oxford: Blackwell, 1990); Bernard Cottret, *Calvin: A Biography* (1995), trans. M. Wallace McDonald (Grand Rapids: Eerdmans, 2000); Bruce Gordon, *Calvin* (New Haven, Conn.: Yale University Press, 2009); W. Robert Godfrey, *John Calvin: Pilgrim and Pastor* (Phillipsburg, N.J.: P&R, 2009); Herman Selderhuis, *John Calvin: A Pilgrim's Life* (Downers Grove, Ill.: InterVarsity Press, 2009). At various points Calvin's biographers disagree with one another, especially where the evidence is thin, for example concerning the exact pattern of his early education.

selection of themes. In particular, I will focus attention on his family life, the events surrounding his conversion, his early ministry, his friendships, and some applications to be made from the life and providences of this magisterial Reformer.

Early Life

Jean Cauvin[2] was born on July 10, 1509, in the town of Noyon, some fifty miles northeast of Paris. He was the third of the four sons of Gérard Cauvin,[3] an official in the local cathedral. Gérard appears to have been a rather difficult man. Calvin's mother, Jeanne, on the other hand, was reputed to be both a physically attractive and pious woman. Calvin later recalled times when she took him on pilgrimages as a small boy. He remembered kissing a relic. However, his mother died when he was about six years old.

It does not require adopting a psychological approach to conclude that this early loss left an indelible impression on Calvin. Simply from the personal point of view, it meant that he lacked the balance of his parents' personalities. The impression certainly arises from Calvin's writings that his relationship with his father was dutiful but not particularly affectionate. That said, it is noteworthy how reticent Calvin was throughout his life to entrust his inner emotional life to writing, and then only within the context of his deepest and most secure friendships.

Two particularly significant privileges arose from Gérard's position as the legal adviser to the chapter of the Noyon Cathedral. The first was that his connections with the Montmor family provided young John with a private education alongside the Montmor children. For a child of Calvin's precocity of mind, this was indeed a privilege. It led, in turn, to his beginning further studies with them in Paris in his early teens.

The ensuing narrative, being introductory in intent, presumes rather than argues for a position on these debates. Readers who wish to investigate the disagreements further will find the different positions identified within the biographies.

2. He did not adopt the formal Latin name Johannes Calvinus until the period in his life when aspirations to scholarship emerged.

3. His brothers were Charles, Anthony, and Francis.

The second was that young Calvin had access to what was essentially the medieval equivalent of a college scholarship. This was accomplished through the practice of granting benefices. Thus, while a student, Calvin was appointed to the "livings" of several congregations. Of course, none of the pastoral responsibilities devolved on him — only the income remaining after someone else had been employed to fulfill those duties. By the time he graduated from the University of Paris, he would be "pastor" of three congregations.

Arriving in Paris in the early 1520s (the precise year is debated), he spent his first few months studying at the Collège de la Marche. Providentially, his instructor there was Mathurin Cordier, one of the finest Latinists of his time. Later in life, Calvin would dedicate his commentary on 1 Thessalonians to him, writing:

> When my father sent me, while yet a boy, to Paris, after I had simply tasted the first elements of the Latin tongue; Providence so ordered it that I had, for a short time, the privilege of having you as my instructor, that I might be taught by you the true method of learning, in such a way that I might be prepared afterwards to make somewhat better proficiency. For, after presiding over the first class with the highest renown, on observing that pupils who had been ambitiously trained up by the other masters, produced nothing but mere show, nothing of solidity, so that they required to be formed by you anew, tired of this annoyance, you that year descended to the fourth class. This, indeed, was what you had in view, but to me it was a singular kindness on the part of God that I happened to have an auspicious commencement of such a course of training....
>
> I derived so much assistance afterwards from your training, that it is with good reason that I acknowledge myself indebted to you for such progress as has since been made. And this I was desirous to testify to posterity, that, if any advantage shall accrue to them from my writings, they shall know that it has in some degree originated with you.[4]

4. John Calvin, "The Author's Epistle Dedicatory to Marturinus Corderius," dated February 17, 1550, in *Commentaries on the Epistles to the Philippians, Colossians, and Thessalonians*, trans. John Pringle (Edinburgh: Calvin Translation Society, 1851), 234.

In that same dedication, Calvin also remembered the darker side of education in the Collège de la Marche. He noted that he was removed from Cordier's tutelage through the less-than-tender care of "an injudicious man, who regulated our studies according to his own pleasure, or rather his caprice."[5]

From there, Calvin soon transferred to the Collège de Montaigu. Father Calvin's aspiration was that his son should enter the priesthood, and de Montaigu was a kind of monastery for teens who intended to become priests.

Calvin recalled two things in particular about college life: first, the food was terrible (he later believed it contributed to the ruin of his own health and that of a number of his fellow students). Second, the college exacted enormous discipline. Classes began at 4 a.m. and continued (with some intermission) until at least 8 p.m. in the winter and 9 p.m. in the summer.

Calvin was a sponge for learning. His preparatory training in Latin, followed by studies in philosophy and rhetoric, led to a spoken and written style marked by simplicity, clarity, delicacy of phrasing, and powerful analytical argument.

Although his masterwork, the *Institutes of the Christian Religion*, evolved into a very large four-book treatise, Calvin early developed an unusual ability in and love for brevity and clarity.[6] Clear communication was one of the passions of his life, whether he was writing letters, theological treatises, or commentaries, or preaching in his native French language. His clear, economic use of language unburdened with complicated phrasing allowed his message to come alive to those who read his works or listened to him preach.

Life at college meant lessons, exercises, and minor inquisitions, as well as bad food. But during that time, Calvin practiced a rigorous self-discipline. Indeed, it may have been at this early time that he

5. Ibid.

6. In his dedication of his Romans commentary to Simon Grynaeus, he recalled a conversation with him in which they were of one mind that "the chief excellency of an expounder consists in lucid brevity." John Calvin, *Commentary on the Epistle of Paul to the Romans*, trans. John Owen (Edinburgh: Calvin Translation Society, 1849), xxiii.

began a practice that would irritate his friends when he became a law student. At the end of every day, he made it a habit to review what he had learned during the day; then, the next morning, he would not rise from bed until he was sure that he remembered everything he had learned the previous day. In many ways, Calvin's self-discipline explains his vast productivity in later life. Though the young man was not yet a believer, he was later conscious of the extent to which God was building into his life habits on which he would draw in order to minister to the glory of God.

By the time Calvin graduated from college, his father had left the cathedral. He was about to be excommunicated in 1528, and, later—were it not for intervention from the family—would have been buried in an unconsecrated grave. In the uncharacteristically autobiographical introduction to his *Commentary on the Psalms*, Calvin guardedly recorded how his father changed his mind and decided that young John should study law rather than prepare for the priesthood. The reason—or at least the one that was given—was, Calvin says, that Gérard now believed the legal profession held much better prospects for his son than the church. So Calvin dutifully went to study law, first at the University of Orleans and later at the University in Bourges.

At this time, Calvin says in the introduction to his *Commentary on the Psalms*, he was "addicted to the papacy." By this, he doubtless meant he had a prejudicial acceptance of and commitment to the medieval Roman Catholic Church with its sacramental way of salvation, and that he lived in conformity to its teaching and obedience to its authority.

Though Calvin does not say so, during his time in college he must have been exposed to the new gospel of the Lutherans. Indeed, he surely would have known of Luther's tracts since they had been under examination by theological professors of the Sorbonne in the early 1520s. No doubt student fascination with the current trends of the academy marked early sixteenth-century Paris as much as it did the Sorbonne of the mid-twentieth century. It is virtually inconceivable that Calvin did not have strong opinions. Indeed, he virtually admits as much when he tells the readers of his Psalms commentary that he was "stubbornly addicted" to the papacy. But this was to change.

Calvin's Conversion

Calvin studied law at the University of Orleans and at the University of Bourges (where he studied Greek literature with Melchior Volmar, with additional classical studies in Paris). As a post-graduate student, Calvin came under the spell of the new humanist movement with its motif of *ad fontes*—returning to the literature of antiquity and to the study of its languages. All of this, in Calvin's case, bore fruit in his earliest publication, a commentary on Seneca's work *De Clementia*, published in 1532. It would be, he hoped, the first step on the ladder of academic advance. He was to be disappointed. Perhaps it would be more accurate to say God providentially would disappoint him. Neither humanism nor a career in academia could answer the needs in Calvin's mind and heart.

Calvin's stubborn allegiance to the Roman Catholic Church now found itself under the pressure of evangelical influences, not least from the entourage of remarkable friends who surrounded him. They shared his passion for learning the old languages, but also—earlier than Calvin—they were developing an interest in and love for the Christian faith in its more primitive New Testament form. Erasmus's Greek New Testament had been published in 1516, and some of Calvin's friends were studying it carefully. They were coming to realize that Luther's views on justification were not, after all, idiosyncratic and heretical, but in fact were founded on basic New Testament teaching.

This "crack" led to the growing realization that the late medieval Roman Catholic Church's theology of salvation could never lead to spiritual certainty. While the church's position was not codified until the Council of Trent (1545–1563), the teaching enunciated by that council simply underlined the current view that the only way to have assurance of salvation was by canonizable levels of holiness or by a special divine revelation. Cardinal Robert Bellarmine, perhaps the most formidable Roman Catholic theologian of the sixteenth century, gave striking expression to this when he claimed that assurance is the greatest of all Protestant heresies.

The way of salvation, according to the Roman church, was dependent first on the grace given at baptism, then progressed through a person's various life experiences governed by the sacraments of the church. One did what one could (*facere quod in se est*) until one's faith was (through the grace of the sacraments) fully formed in perfect love for God (*fides formata caritate*). At this point, "by grace" (i.e. through the sacramental system) a person became actually righteous in himself and therefore could be accounted righteous in God's sight. Justification in this sense was claimed to be "by grace," but it was *not* "by faith alone." Rome regarded any different teaching (such as Luther's doctrine of the justification of the ungodly in his ungodliness) as a "legal fiction." Thus, for Rome, grace involved the infusion, not the imputation, of righteousness; sinners were justified because grace made them justifiable.

This system rendered assurance virtually impossible. How could one know one had "done enough"? The system left ordinary men and women without certainty of faith. Without assurance, the people were bound to the sacramental system of the church, fair game for the sale of indulgences, and deprived of all joy in salvation.

Judging by the emphasis Calvin would later place (in various contexts) on certainty in the Christian life, it seems likely that coming to an assured knowledge of God and the forgiveness of sins in Christ was a major element in his conversion. Calvin and his young friends were beginning to read in the pages of their Greek New Testaments of ordinary men and women who abounded in pardon, assurance, joy, and freedom, certain that nothing could separate them from the love of God in Christ Jesus. In the New Testament, people experienced the love of God poured into their hearts by the Holy Spirit from the very beginning of the life of faith.

Some of Calvin's friends were beginning to speak more openly about their new discoveries. One of them was Calvin's cousin, Pierre Robert Olivétan, whose diligence in study rivaled Calvin's own. Eventually Olivétan would translate the Bible into French — and his cousin John would write the preface (1534). Calvin also was beginning to move in the circles of reform of which King Francis's sister, Marguerite of Navarre, was the guardian, and which included her confessor, Gérard Roussel.

Another friend was Nicholas Cop, who would deliver the Rector's Address at the University of Paris in November 1533. Theodore Beza, Calvin's colleague and successor in Geneva, and an early biographer, believed that Calvin himself was the author of the speech. The speech is interesting for its combination of the old and the new. It expresses the movement toward New Testament Christianity; but while there is protest, there is not yet Protestantism. In any event, Calvin fled Paris in the maelstrom that followed. In 1534, the incident of the Placards (when anti-Roman placards were posted throughout Paris—including, reportedly, on the king's bedchamber door) meant that Paris was a city permanently closed to Calvin. He was beginning to preach now and even to write model sermons, but all of the implications of the pathway on which he had started were not yet clear.

What happened to bring him fully into the Reformation movement? All we know from Calvin's own hand is that God subdued him to docility by a sudden (or unexpected) conversion. It is tempting to think that he was referring to what we would call his "conversion experience," but perhaps it is a description only of its beginnings, in which his stubborn spirit became teachable. Certainly his full confession of being an "évangélique" would wait for his forfeiture of his benefices in the realization that since others were giving their lives for the gospel he must not remain hidden, even if he still aspired to the life of a scholar. He had, at last, grasped what would be a central motif in his developed theology—everything we need is provided for us in Christ, plus nothing.[7]

Scholars have discussed what passage of Scripture most influenced Calvin's conversion. Ford Lewis Battles, who translated the 1960 English edition of the *Institutes*, argued that it was Romans 1:18–32 because of the way the *Institutes* is divided into the knowledge of God the Creator and the knowledge of God the Savior in Jesus Christ.[8] Romans 1 certainly did have a profound influence on Calvin's

7. See his exposition in *Institutes of the Christian Religion*, ed. John T. McNeill, trans. Ford Lewis Battles (Louisville: Westminster John Knox, 1960), Book II, Chapter 16.

8. See F. L. Battles, *The Piety of John Calvin* (Grand Rapids: Baker, 1978), 48.

theology. But Calvin may have been more influenced by Paul's letter to the Philippians. Certainly he keeps returning in his writings to the theme that the Christian loses everything for Christ but gains everything through Him. Whether we live or die, Christ is ours. From one standpoint, Calvin lost everything by giving himself in faith to Jesus Christ.

By whatever means, whether slow or sudden, Calvin's conversion took place. His stubborn addiction to the papacy was broken and his heart subdued. From that time forward, the great motto of his life became, "Lord, I offer my heart to Thee, promptly and sincerely." His personal symbol (apparently designed by himself) was an open hand with a heart between the letters J and C. Calvin, still in his twenties, now belonged to Christ.

He was part of a widespread movement involving many young people. It is easy to forget just how young they actually were. Many of them were arrested for their faith; numbers were executed. One of those who was put to death was Calvin's landlord in Paris. Calvin's own room was searched. He and his friends became hunted criminals. By the time he was twenty-six, Calvin was on the run; he had become a pilgrim and would live the rest of his life as a refugee. His ambition remained solitude and study, but now there also burned within him a passion to serve his fellow believers.

In 1536, the *Institutes of the Christian Religion* came from the press. It was a small, six-chapter paperback at first, but over the years it grew into the substantial work of theology with which we are familiar today. The final edition was printed in 1559 (French translation, 1560).

Calvin's first concern was merely to produce a work that would edify Christians and, to some extent, serve as an apology for the Reformed faith. In the face of criticism and hostility, he wanted to prove that fidelity to Scripture characterized the new evangelicals. He wrote an extensive prefatory letter to King Francis I of France, defending the Reformation against a whole series of false accusations.

Calvin's Ministry

Calvin was on the run. In a relatively short time, he traversed Europe, moving through Italy and Switzerland. He returned briefly to Noyon in

1536 to gather members of his family and some friends to accompany him to Strasbourg, where he could continue his scholarly life. But they could not go directly there because of troop movements. Instead, they decided to enter Switzerland near Geneva. The plan was to stay for a night or two before moving on to Strasbourg.

Paradoxically, one of Calvin's friends, Louis du Tillet,[9] let slip that the young man traveling through Geneva was in fact the author of the *Institutes of the Christian Religion*. William Farel, who had come to Geneva to lead the work of reformation, sought Calvin out. Geneva had recently embraced the Reformation, but it had not yet been transformed into an evangelical city, and Farel believed Calvin was the man Geneva needed. Calvin resisted Farel's appeal. The story is best told in his own words:

> I had resolved to continue in the same privacy and obscurity, until at length William Farel detained me at Geneva, not so much by counsel and exhortation, as by a dreadful imprecation, which I felt to be as if God had from heaven laid his mighty hand upon me to arrest me. As the most direct road to Strasburg, to which I then intended to retire, was shut up by the wars, I had resolved to pass quickly by Geneva, without staying longer than a single night in that city. A little before this, Popery had been driven from it by the exertions of the excellent person whom I have named, and Peter Viret; but matters were not yet brought to a settled state, and the city was divided into unholy and dangerous factions. Then an individual who now basely apostatised and returned to the Papists, discovered me and made me known to others. Upon this, Farel, who burned with an extraordinary zeal to advance the gospel, immediately strained every nerve to detain me. And after having learned that my heart was set upon devoting myself to private studies for which I wished to keep myself free from other pursuits, and finding that he gained nothing by entreaties, he proceeded to utter an imprecation that God would curse my retirement, and the tranquillity of the

9. "Paradoxically," since du Tillet later returned to the Roman Catholic Church. In God's providence, the remarkable ministry of Calvin in Geneva was thus in part effected by someone who rejected the ministry for which Calvin stood.

> studies which I sought, if I should withdraw and refuse to give assistance, when the necessity was so urgent. By this imprecation I was so stricken with terror, that I desisted from the journey which I had undertaken.[10]

So Calvin stayed in Geneva. On more than one occasion in the years that followed, he might have believed that by staying in Geneva he was experiencing the curse of God. The Genevans had separated from the Roman church, but they were not "set apart for the gospel of God" (Rom. 1:1).

The ministry there was far from being a sinecure. The early years (1536–1538) proved to be a nightmare. Many were opposed to the preaching of the Word of God. During Calvin's sermons, there were all kinds of unseemly noises, as well as irritating chattering and mockery of the preacher. Even later, the Register of the Consistory of Geneva reads like a chronicle of spiritual indifference on the part of church members.

As the Word of God came forth from the pulpit in Geneva, stressing the urgency of faith, repentance, and sanctification, opposition intensified. People would shoot their guns outside Calvin's residence while he was trying to sleep. They would set their dogs on him in the street—indeed, some of them named their dogs after him (without affection). Near-constant friction developed between the ministers and numbers of the citizens, and also between the ministers and the city government.

The crisis point was reached on Easter Sunday of 1538, when Calvin and other ministers preached but then refused to serve the Lord's Supper. They were told to leave the city when replacements could be found. A few days later, they were told to leave without delay. By the end of the week, Calvin was an exile again. In his own words, "I was banished from Geneva."[11]

---

10. John Calvin, *Commentary on the Book of Psalms*, trans. James Anderson (Edinburgh: Calvin Translation Society, 1845), xlii–xliii.

11. Ibid.

It is not difficult to imagine how low Calvin must have sunk at that point. "Naturally of a timid, soft, and pusillanimous disposition,"[12] and now with what must have felt like a disastrously brief ministry, it is not surprising that he had little taste to begin again. What he most needed was a wise minister to come alongside him, put his hand on his shoulder, and say: "Join me here. Watch how we do things here. Pick up the vibrations of what ministry means. Learn all over again. We will give you opportunity, we will encourage you, we will pray for you, and we will minister to you."

That is exactly what Martin Bucer, the seasoned pastor of Strasbourg, did for Calvin. But Calvin did not bend easily. Like Farel before him, Bucer found Calvin resistant to his proposal. Bruised and wounded, he simply wanted to go back to his books. But Bucer had exactly the biblical model to bind Calvin's conscience—Jonah:

> That most excellent servant of Christ, Martin Bucer, employing a similar kind of remonstrance and protestation as that to which Farel had recourse before, drew me back to a new station. Alarmed by the example of Jonas, which he set before me, I still continued in the work of teaching.[13]

Bucer encouraged Calvin to lead a congregation of French refugees, which numbered about five hundred. That may well be the ideal size for a church: everyone can know everyone else in such a congregation; the pastor can know his sheep by name; everyone can know the pastor; and a wide variety of gifts is likely to be present. Calvin grew as he preached God's Word and ministered to his new people. He also thought through many issues of worship and church life.

Calvin was single, and seems to have had little thought of marrying and a great desire for privacy. His friends, however, were determined to find him a wife. Calvin respected their authority, as they introduced him to one woman after another. Indeed, they went so far as to fix a wedding date for Calvin and a young lady of their choice. Calvin might have married were it not for the fact that he learned more about

12. Ibid.
13. Ibid.

the lady. When he did, he wrote that he would have needed to have lost his mind to have married her!

In August 1540, Calvin married Idelette de Bure, the widow of an Anabaptist convert. She had a little boy and girl. They enjoyed a happy, but short, marriage. In July 1542, she bore him a son, Jacques. He was a premature baby and died in infancy. In the grief of that loss, Calvin wrote about the Fatherhood of his God and bowed to confess that He knows best what is for the good of His children. But the sense of loss remained with him throughout his life.

Although Calvin's closest male friend at this time was his brother Antoine, who lived in the house, there is little doubt that Idelette was his heart. Her health was precarious, however, and after a few years of illness, she died in 1549. Calvin deeply grieved her loss. He wrote to Viret with stark simplicity: "I have been bereaved of the best companion of my life...she was the faithful helper of my ministry."[14]

The Strasbourg period was perhaps the happiest in Calvin's life. But in the sixteenth century, no one was ever far from pain and loss. In one year of his sojourn there (1538), Calvin nursed his friend Farel's nephew prior to his death from the plague, and lost his friend and blind fellow pastor Elie Courault, who had worked with him in Geneva, and his brilliant cousin Olivétan. But exercising iron discipline in this season of great loss, Calvin accomplished two significant things. While growing into pastoral ministry, he revised the *Institutes*, expanding it from a small paperback to a large book. He also conceived what we might call "The Calvin project"—a one-man production of a biblically rooted theology (the *Institutes*) accompanied by a series of commentaries on the entire New Testament. He began with the book of Romans.

Calvin realized that the new Reformation church needed doctrine that could be taught and applied clearly, and that men and women needed to understand how the message of the gospel derives from and is shaped by Scripture. At the same time, he saw how the Scriptures could be expounded in the form of commentaries. It is remarkable,

14. John Calvin, *Letters of John Calvin*, trans. David Constable, ed. Jules Bonnet (Philadelphia: Presbyterian Board of Publication, 1858), 2:216.

given the workload he carried (preaching five, six, or seven times each week, lecturing, writing letters, working on various writing projects, studying, attending many meetings, counseling), Calvin almost succeeded in completing his New Testament exposition (only 2 and 3 John and Revelation lack comment). Thus, as people studied Scripture, Calvin reasoned, they would have two kinds of works to help them: a volume of theology that would teach them the contours of the gospel and provide a road map, and commentaries that would demonstrate how the doctrine was both constituted and confirmed from divine revelation. The goal of the project was to produce all-Bible and all-doctrine Christians, whose lives were transformed by the renewing of their minds.

Although Calvin was exiled from Geneva during this time, he continued to have contact with the Genevans, even though the relationship remained strained and difficult. At one point, the Genevans received a letter from the Roman Catholic Cardinal Jacopo Sadoleto. He was deeply scathing about the Reformation, but—in his own view, graciously—invited the Genevans to return to the fold of Rome. They had no local resources adequate to answer Sadoleto, so they asked Calvin to respond. His reply to the cardinal is one of the small masterpieces of Reformation writing. Sadoleto had spoken about the judgment seat. Calvin's response expounded the privileges of grace in the confession an evangelical believer could make at that judgment seat.

In 1540, he was asked to return to Geneva. His response was predictable. He wrote to Farel on March 29, 1540: "Rather would I submit to death a hundred times than to that cross on which one had to perish daily one thousand times over."[15] Nevertheless, he eventually agreed to go, but only on loan for six months. He returned to the pulpit, made a few remarks, and then began preaching on the same passage he had left off preaching on a few years before. In a profound sense, it was the first day of the rest of his life.

Calvin remained in Geneva and gave himself to its people and its transformation over the quarter century that followed, until his death in 1564. All was not plain sailing. But Calvin was a more seasoned pastor

15. Calvin, *Letters*, 1:75.

now. He knew better how to lead, how to pastor, how to care, and, not least, how to endure to the end. The result was what John Knox called "The most perfect school of Christ since the days of the apostles."

Lessons from the Life of Calvin

During most of his time in Geneva, Calvin lived on the edge. He tended to do that, but the edge in this case was enormous political pressure. He was not a citizen of Geneva; he was a refugee until a few years before he died. He had no formal political power. In addition, for many years he faced an underlying hostility to his presence and his ministry. As late as the 1550s, Calvin remained convinced he would have to leave Geneva again. Only in 1555 did the city fathers give the church the right of excommunication, thereby ceding spiritual authority. He also labored under great personal pressure due to attacks from his enemies, some of whom had originally enticed him to come back to Geneva.

There were other trials, too, such as "The Servetus Affair" in 1553. Michael Servetus—who had a history with Calvin—had already been condemned and placed under sentence of death for heresy throughout Europe, and he soon was charged in Geneva, especially for his anti-trinitarian teaching. A deeply unstable figure, he seems to have come to Geneva deliberately to challenge Calvin to refute his views. He was offered the opportunity to return to France to be tried as a heretic, but he begged to be tried in Geneva, perhaps hoping that Calvin would refuse to deal with the issue in the light of the ongoing insecurity of his position. Nonetheless, the Council of Geneva convicted Servetus of heresy and ordered him to be burned at the stake. Calvin argued for a more humane death, but his request was refused.

Another difficulty Calvin had to deal with was Jerome Bolsec, a strange, unstable former Carmelite father. He was a physician (and spy) in the court of Renée of Ferrara. He appeared in Geneva in 1551. While he expressed appreciation for much of Calvin's teaching, he had a deep distaste for the biblical doctrine of predestination.

On Fridays, Calvin met in what was essentially a group Bible study for local ministers and others, known as the congrégation. At one of those meetings, Bolsec brought up the subject of predestination, attacking Calvin full-on. He did not realize that Calvin was at the meeting and was listening to the whole performance. Needless to say, Calvin was not greatly impressed or pleased. Bolsec became an implacable enemy from that time on. He wrote much against the Reformer that was libelous and destructive. Calvin was haunted by such attacks, as well as the less sophisticated but ongoing opposition to the gospel and the Reformation.

How, then, was the work in Geneva transformed from a quasi-political reformation to a genuine gospel reformation? Two things account for this.

First, prayer changed the city. One of the first things Calvin did on his return from Strasbourg was to institute a weekly day of prayer. While there was regular preaching each weekday, Wednesdays were set aside for prayer from 8 a.m. to 10 a.m. At these times, as well as in the regular private prayers of the congregation and the regular prayers in the worship services, the people and the ministers prayed for the benediction of God on the city and on the growing number of churches that were being planted outside of Geneva.

The second thing that transformed Geneva was the ministry of the Word of God. Sermons were preached on Sunday mornings and afternoons. On weekdays, Calvin preached three times during the week (and when his strength allowed it, he preached every day). Beza says about a thousand people crowded into the cathedral in Geneva to listen to this frail, asthmatic man as he preached the Word of God. He worked the Word of God like a potter into the clay of God's people in Geneva, sometimes preaching ten times a week, perhaps forty minutes or more each time. Besides that, he gave three lectures on the Old Testament to students each week, went to consistory meetings on Thursdays, and participated in the congrégation. (Imagine having Calvin at your group Bible study!)

Clearly Calvin's mind was always at work, always fertile. But his life was not only a constant round of sermon preparation, prayer, lectures, writing, and conferences. Earlier in his ministry life, in a note to Farel (1539), he wrote:

> When the present messenger wished to carry along with him the beginning of my book, there were still twenty leaves, which it required me to revise. In addition, there was the public lecture and I also had to preach; four letters were also to be written; some disputes to settle, and to reply to more than ten interruptions in the meantime. You will therefore excuse if my letter should be both brief and inaccurate.[16]

With such enormous pressure, it makes sense that several years later (1551), Calvin wrote to Heinrich Bullinger, "I am so much exhausted by constant writing, and so greatly broken down by fatigue, that I frequently feel an almost positive aversion to writing a letter."[17] At that point, Calvin was given secretaries to take down his dictation.

Space forbids further elaboration of the life of this remarkable man whom God raised up. Calvin was far from perfect. But often the measure of a man is to be assessed not so much by his height as by the obstacles he overcomes in order to grow. By that canon of assessment, Calvin was even more remarkable. During most of his ministry, he was a sick man. He suffered from malaria and tuberculosis; he also had a heart problem, gout, migraines, and kidney stones (the remedies being almost worse than the stones themselves). He had digestive problems and often suffered from insomnia. Yet Calvin was constantly critical of himself and his shortcomings. He lived physically and spiritually on the edge. At times he could be irritable. It was a wonderful reality, then, to this tightly wound man, living under such great pressure, that Jesus Christ was so kind.

That thought—the kindness of Christ—serves as a fitting reminder of Calvin's deep Christ-centeredness. It would be difficult to exaggerate the extent to which this was true. He had found in Christ the wisdom, righteousness, sanctification, and redemption he needed. Indeed, he found all he needed in Christ, and urged others to search nowhere else. It is therefore not difficult to imagine that he may indeed have been involved in the writing of the only hymn (in distinction from metricized psalms) that has ever been attributed to him:

16. Ibid., 1:132.
17. Ibid., 2:304.

I greet Thee, who my sure Redeemer art,
My only trust and Savior of my heart,
Who pain didst undergo for my poor sake;
I pray Thee from our hearts all cares to take.

Thou art the King of mercy and of grace,
Reigning omnipotent in every place;
So come, O King, and our whole being sway;
Shine on us with the light of Thy pure day.

Thou art the life, by which alone we live,
And all our substance and our strength receive;
Sustain us by Thy faith and by Thy power,
And give us strength in every trying hour.

Thou hast the true and perfect gentleness,
No harshness hast Thou and no bitterness;
O grant to us the grace we find in Thee,
That we may dwell in perfect unity.

Our hope is in no other save in Thee;
Our faith is built upon Thy promise free;
Lord, give us peace, and make us calm and sure,
That in Thy strength we evermore endure.

CHAPTER 2

Calvin the Reformer

IAN HAMILTON

What T. F. Torrance wrote in praise of Karl Barth could, with even more propriety, be applied to John Calvin: "There arise from time to time, men who tower above the immediate context, not only because they are men of genius, but because they are so steeped in the history of thought, that they obtain a breadth of comprehension reaching out beyond the Zeitgeist of any one age."[1] Such, by the grace of God, was Calvin.

Any discussion of Calvin the Reformer needs to appreciate both the precarious political situation in which Calvin pursued his reforming initiatives and the internecine rivalries within the Reformed camp that continually frustrated his attempts to advance his particular vision for reform. Throughout the nearly thirty years that he engaged in the reform movement, all of Calvin's reforming activity was carried out in the midst of wars and rumors of wars. Protestantism was internally divided and vulnerable to changing political alliances. Threats of invasion, shifting political alliances, imperial politics, and the suspicion (and worse) of fellow Reformers was the context in which Calvin strove to defend and promote the cause of reform.

In addition, during the last fifteen years of his life in particular, Calvin suffered from a multitude of painful, often debilitating, illnesses. He never had the luxury of pursuing the work of reformation either with good health or with the unified support of his fellow Protestants. Whether battling theological opponents such as Jerome

1. T. F. Torrance, in *Karl Barth: An Introduction to His Early Theology, 1910–1931*, quoted in R. S. Wallace, *Calvin, Geneva and the Reformation* (Grand Rapids: Baker, 1988), 237–38.

Bolsec, Sebastian Castellio, and Michael Servetus, or seeking to defuse theological controversies with Berne, Zurich, and England, Calvin could not forget for one moment that the cause of Christ was often, humanly speaking, hanging like a thread—but as Samuel Rutherford would later say, "a thread of Christ's spinning."[2]

It would be a mistake of the first order, then, to suppose that Calvin strode the Reformed scene like some kind of invincible colossus. He was without doubt "the theologian" of the Reformed churches (as Philip Melanchthon called him), but even when it seemed that he had outmaneuvered and theologically defeated his enemies in Geneva, he still wrote to Johannes Wolf in late 1555:

> Believe me, I had fewer troubles with Servetus and have now with Westphal and his like than I have with those who are close at hand, whose numbers are beyond reckoning and whose passions are irreconcilable. If one could choose, it would be better to be burned once by the papists than to be plagued for eternity by one's neighbours. They do not allow me a moment's rest, although they can clearly see that I am collapsing under the burden of work, troubled by endless sad occurrences, and disturbed by intrusive demands. My comfort is that death will soon take me from this all too difficult service.[3]

Calvin never had a consciously developed strategy for reform. As the years passed, he embraced opportunities for reform as they presented themselves, persuaded that the Lord had equipped him to take the struggle for reformation beyond the confines of his adopted city. To that end, Calvin used every providential means at his disposal: five times he revised his *Institutes of the Christian Religion*; he wrote biblical commentaries and tracts (often dedicated to important national and imperial figures); he preached incessantly; he penned letters to monarchs, church dignitaries, fledgling churches, and "ordinary Christians"; and he encouraged men to take the gospel, at

2. *The Letters of Samuel Rutherford,* (Edinburgh: Banner of Truth Trust, 2003), http://www.archive.org/stream/letters ofrevsamu00ruth/lettersofrevsamu00ruth_djvu.txt (accessed February 2, 2010).

3. Calvin to Johannes Wolf, Dec. 25, 1555, quoted in Bruce Gordon, *Calvin* (New Haven, Conn.: Yale University Press, 2009), 233.

huge personal risk, throughout Europe and beyond. In all of this, he pursued Protestant church unity with such passion and persistence that he literally wore himself out. To his enemies in Geneva he may have been *ille gallus* ("that Frenchman"), but Calvin's Christianity transcended national boundaries. Geneva may have been his "first love" and France his motherland, but Europe, and indeed the world, was his mission field.

By temperament, Calvin was self-confessedly shy. He described himself as "a poor, timid, scholar" and longed for a life of quiet study and theological reflection: "In short," he wrote, "while my one great object was to live in seclusion without being known...God brought me forth to public notice."[4] Whereas Martin Luther revelled in debate and controversy, Calvin naturally shrunk from public disagreement. Yet he became, along with Heinrich Bullinger, the leading Reformer of his age.

The purpose of this chapter is to try to explain the factors, internal and external, that transformed Calvin from a shy and timid scholar, engulfed by enemies, criticized by friends, and afflicted with numerous physical illnesses, into a passionate, persistent, and international Reformer.

A Man Subdued by God

In the first place, we need to appreciate the spiritual dynamic that captivated Calvin. He was, in his own words, a man subdued by God (*Deus subegit*).[5] He was not his own. This, I believe, is the key to understanding Calvin the Reformer. He was motivated by the sense that God had captured him and commissioned him to serve the cause of truth in an age dominated by lies and confusion.

It was his deep sense that his life belonged to Jesus Christ alone that brought Calvin back to Geneva in 1541 to continue the work of reformation, three years after he had been dismissed by the Genevan authorities. In 1540, when Calvin's friends urged him to return to Geneva, he gave them an "over my dead body" response. He wrote to

4. In *CO* 31:21, quoted in Gordon, *Calvin*, 47.
5. *Commentary* on Psalms, preface.

Pierre Viret: "I read that passage in your letter, certainly not without a smile, where you shew (sic) so much concern about my health, and recommend Geneva on that ground. Why could you not have said at the cross? For it would have been far preferable to perish once for all than to be tormented again in that place of torture. Therefore, my dear Viret, if you wish well to me, make no mention of such a proposal."[6] Yet he returned the next year. Why? He wrote to William Farel in August 1541: "As to my intended course of proceeding, this is my present feeling: had I the choice at my own disposal, nothing would be less agreeable to me than to follow your advice. But when I remember that I am not my own, I offer up my heart, presented as a sacrifice to the Lord.... Therefore I submit my will and my affections, subdued and held-fast, to the obedience of God."[7] The sense of being *Deus subegit* never left Calvin. His personal emblem was a picture of a flaming heart held up in a hand with the inscription *Cor meum tibi offero, Domine, prompte et sincere* ("My heart I offer to Thee, O Lord, promptly and sincerely").

I am conscious that the Lord also uses external providences to confirm to us, and sometimes to press upon us, His will. Calvin, subdued by God, was also probably encouraged to return to Geneva by his sense of disillusionment with the colloquies at Hagenau and then at Worms in 1540–1541. The failure of these colloquies, allied to Martin Bucer's willingness to seek a theological compromise with Rome, persuaded Calvin that his time in Strasbourg was perhaps coming to an end. He longed for the unity of Protestant churches, but not at any cost. In returning to Geneva, Calvin was turning his back on the "Strasbourg approach."[8]

Calvin did not set out to be a Reformer; rather, in God's providence, he found himself spiritually, intellectually, and theologically equipped to give the Reformed cause the leadership it cried out for, and he was willing to provide that leadership. When he urged men to take up the cross and follow Christ no matter the cost, he spoke and wrote as a

6. John Calvin, *Tracts and Letters* (Edinburgh: Banner of Truth, 2009), 4:187.
7. Ibid., 4:280–81.
8. Gordon, *Calvin*, 101.

man who had done that himself. There was credibility in Calvin's pleas for reformation!

Doctrinal Motivations

Second, Calvin the Reformer was doctrinally animated by his desire to recover the true worship of God and the truth concerning salvation by grace alone through faith alone in Christ alone for the church. In his letter to Emperor Charles V, prefacing his treatise *The Necessity of Reforming the Church* (1543), Calvin sought to explain why he and others, following Luther, were pursuing the work of reformation: "If it be inquired, then, by what things chiefly the Christian religion has a standing amongst us, and maintains its truth, it will be found that the following two not only occupy the principal place, but comprehend under them all the other parts, and consequently the whole substance of Christianity, viz., a knowledge, first of the mode in which God is duly worshipped; and, secondly, of the source from which salvation is to be obtained."[9] The ignorance and abuse of the church's worship and the ignorance of God's revealed way of salvation compelled Calvin to pursue reformation with unremitting zeal.

Throughout his ministry, Calvin was involved in a "worship war" (nothing is new), and he labored to restore to the church the pure worship of God, that is, worship shaped and styled alone by Holy Scripture (though, as we will see, Calvin was relatively indifferent to the precise mechanics of worship). For Calvin, nothing was more important than God being worshiped as He decreed in His Word. The "will worship," the ritual and superstition of Romanist worship, was an abomination to Calvin. What passed for worship was no worship at all. In his reply to Cardinal Sadoleto (1539), one of the brilliant defenses of the Reformation, Calvin wrote:

> There is nothing more perilous to our salvation than a preposterous and perverse worship of God.... But since God not only regards as fruitless, but also plainly abominates, whatever we undertake from zeal to His worship, if at variance with His command, what

9. Calvin, *Tracts and Letters,* 1:126.

> do we gain by a contrary course? The words of God are clear and distinct, "Obedience is better than sacrifice." "In vain do they worship me, teaching for doctrines the commandments of men" (1 Sam. xv. 22; Matth. xv 9). Every addition to His word, especially in this matter, is a lie. Mere 'will worship' is vanity. This is the decision, and when once the judge has decided, it is no longer time to debate.[10]

This is the "regulative principle" of worship. Calvin did not expound this principle woodenly (cf. *Inst.* 4.10.30), but he did proclaim it passionately. God's holy honor required it. It matters how we worship God!

No less was Calvin animated in his pursuit of reformation by his desire to recover the sovereignty of God and His grace in salvation. Calvin was appalled by the semi-Pelagianism of Rome's teaching on salvation. This is perhaps nowhere more passionately expressed by Calvin than in his *Reply to Sadoleto*: "You, in the first place, touch upon justification by faith, the first and keenest subject of controversy between us. Is this a knotty and useless question? Wherever the knowledge of it is taken away, the glory of Christ is extinguished, religion abolished, the Church destroyed, and the hope of salvation utterly overthrown."[11]

In our age of doctrinal indifferentism, how greatly we need to be confronted afresh by the Reformers' passion for the truth "once delivered to the saints" (Jude 3), truth they were willing to live and die for. We who claim to be the spiritual heirs of Calvin are often reluctant to lose our pulpits for the cause of gospel truth. Our often-pusillanimous responses to the disfiguring of the gospel in our day would be incomprehensible to Calvin.

A Passion for Peace and Unity

Third, Calvin's passion for peace and unity in the church permeated all his reforming initiatives. Calvin emerged at a time when Protestants were visibly and acrimoniously divided, and from the outset he sought

10. Ibid., 1:34.
11. Ibid., 1:41.

to heal those breaches. In his justly famous letter to Thomas Cranmer, then Archbishop of Canterbury, Calvin wrote: "This other thing also is to be ranked among the chief evils of our time, viz., that the churches are so divided, that human fellowship is scarcely now in any repute among us, far less that Christian intercourse which all make a profession of, but few sincerely practise.... Thus it is that the members of the Church being severed, the body lies bleeding. So much does this concern me, that, could I be of any service, I would not grudge to cross even ten seas, if need were, on account of it."[12] Calvin would not have comprehended how Reformed Christians today can be so indifferent to Christ's "bleeding body."

Calvin's pursuit of visible church unity (which was more doctrinal than organizational) was seen first in his tireless attempts to find a solution to the vexed question of the presence of Christ in the sacrament of the Lord's Supper. In seeking a solution that would satisfy Zwinglians and Lutherans, he was zealous yet flexible. His flexibility is seen in his commitment to the *Consensus Tigurinus* (1549), in which he and Bullinger reached agreement on twenty-four articles relating to the Supper. Calvin had long desired that his conviction that the sacraments were divinely ordained instruments for conferring grace (*sacramenta conferunt gratiam*) would become the standard view of the Reformed churches, so he wanted this language in the *Consensus.* Bullinger, however, prevailed, and the word *instrumentum* was not included in the text. Two months later, however (perhaps desiring to have his view more clearly represented or having second thoughts), Calvin added two articles to clarify his teaching. Remarkably, Bullinger concurred. Diarmaid MacCulloch remarks that the *Consensus Tigurinus* is "a tribute to both Calvin's and Bullinger's common sense and ability to be gracious when circumstances cried out for it."[13]

Gordon maintains that the *Consensus Tigurinus* showed that Bullinger had "tamed" Calvin, persuading him to lay aside the ideal for the reasonable.[14] But while it is certainly true that Calvin greatly

12. Ibid., 5:347–48.

13. Diarmaid MacCulloch, *The Reformation* (New York: Viking, 2003), 244.

14. Gordon, *Calvin*, 179.

respected Bullinger, it is more likely that his respect for his friend, allied to his instinctive catholicity, led him to embrace the *Consensus* in the interests of Protestant unity.

Calvin hoped, and perhaps even thought, that the *Consensus* would be welcomed both by the other churches in the Swiss Confederation and by Melanchthon and the majority of the Lutherans. In thinking this, especially with regard to the Lutherans, Calvin was expressing more hope than sense—as his later pamphlet war with Joachim Westphal revealed only too clearly. In so passionately pursuing the reformation and unity of the Protestant churches, Calvin appeared less than fully to appreciate just how the other Swiss churches, and especially the Lutherans, viewed his theology (especially on the sacraments and predestination). Most charitably we can say that he was so passionately committed to Protestant unity that he assumed other evangelicals were as willing as he was to compromise on confessional language, and even doctrine, in order to achieve visible unity among Christ's churches.

Calvin was especially perplexed in his pursuit of Protestant unity with Melanchthon. He hoped and perhaps even assumed that Melanchthon would publicly approve the *Consensus* and support him in his quest for "the Protestant world to speak with one voice."[15] In his exasperation, Calvin wrote a somewhat stinging letter to his friend:

> Though you shrink from noisy contests, yet you know what Paul prescribes by his example to all the servants of Christ. Certainly you cannot desire praise for greater moderation than that which was evidenced in him. When he then, who was endowed with so much forbearance, passed intrepidly through seditions, we cannot give way where the circumstances in our times are by no means so painful. But, in one word, you should maturely consider whether your too obstinate a silence may not leave a stain on your reputation in the years of posterity.

Calvin then added, "If a means of pacification is sought for, our only hope lies in a conference; which I doubt not but you desire, but which I could wish that you called for more courageously."[16] The

15. Ibid., 248.
16. Calvin, *Tracts and Letters*, 6:337.

conference that Calvin hoped for never materialized. Melanchthon kept silent.

Calvin also pursued peace and unity among the Protestant churches by his pastorally wise advice to churches pursuing scriptural purity in worship. In his letter *To the English at Frankfurt* in January 1555, Calvin urged them to recognize the perilous times they were living in and to lay aside "contentions about forms of prayer and ceremonies." Calvin was not saying that these matters are of no importance. He was, however, reminding the English exiles not to behave "as if you were at ease and in a season of tranquillity, and thus throwing an obstacle in the way of your coalescing in one body of worshippers," which, he added, "is really too unreasonable."[17]

Calvin was clearly sympathetic to the concern of the exiles. He speaks of the ceremonies they were being required to submit to as "silly things"; however, "silly things that might be tolerated." He tells the exiles that regarding matters such as "external rites," he himself is "indulgent and pliable"; though he is quick to add, "I do not deem it expedient always to comply with the foolish captiousness of those who will not give up a single point of their usual routine." Yes, the exiles, and all believers, should be aiming "at something purer" (that is, a church shaped by the teaching of Holy Scripture alone). But this, Calvin is quick to acknowledge, will take time, and "faults" will not "be corrected on the first day."[18]

The same patience is seen in his letter to Edward Seymour, duke of Somerset (Lord Protector of England from 1547 to 1549). In that letter, Calvin expresses his concern that the Reformation in England was proceeding all too slowly, but continues, "I willingly acknowledge that we must observe moderation, and that overdoing is neither discreet nor useful; indeed, that forms of worship need to be accommodated to the condition and tastes of the people. But the corruptions of Satan and of Antichrist must not be admitted under that pretext."[19]

17. Ibid., 6:117–18.
18. Ibid., 6:118.
19. Ibid., 5:193.

Calvin's moderation, however, did not extend to the "Nicodemites," who embraced the evangelical faith but hid their gospel allegiance by conforming to the worship practices of the Roman church. Unlike Bucer, who thought that a compromise could possibly be reached with the Roman church, Calvin was adamant that true believers must leave "the Great Harlot." He viewed Rome as "Babylon," incapable of internal reform. As such, all believers must totally reject her and come out from her. Calvin's opposition to the Nicodemites was criticized by some Reformed believers as too harsh and "inexpedient." But for Calvin, the issue first and foremost was not what would best further the cause of reform, but what would best and most honor God. He believed it would be right to leave the Roman church even if that decision did not politically or ecclesiastically appear to advance the gospel—truth must always trump consequences.

Commitment to holy moderation and accommodation, however, essentially marked Calvin's pursuit of wider church unity among the Reformed. There is a striking passage in the *Institutes* (4.10.30) where Calvin notes that God's instructions for worship in Scripture do not "prescribe in detail what we ought to do"—because he foresaw that this depended upon the state of the times, and he did not deem one form suitable for all ages. While acknowledging that "we ought not to charge into innovation rashly, suddenly, for insufficient cause," Calvin concludes, "But love will best judge what may hurt or edify; and if we let love be our guide, all will be safe."[20] The example Calvin instances is "kneeling when solemn prayers are being said." However, his readiness to "let love be our guide" is a reflection of his accommodating nature and a challenge to his modern heirs to exhibit the same ecclesiological breadth of spirit.

In pursuit of Protestant church unity, Calvin "travelled extensively, frequently visiting Berne, Zurich and Basle, as well as journeying further afield to Frankfurt and Strasbourg."[21] He received a constant flow of visitors from all over Europe and wrote letters to refugees, statesmen, princes, struggling saints, pastors awaiting execution, bishops, and at

20. *Institutes*, 4.10.30.

21. Gordon, *Calvin*, 251.

least one archbishop. He wrote to Marguerite of Navarre. He dedicated the 1536 edition of the *Institutes* to Francis I, king of France, which "signalled Calvin's belief in the power of rhetorical argument in addressing leaders."[22]

I would guess that this element in Calvin's reforming zeal would surprise, and perhaps embarrass, many Reformed Christians today. We tend to be so wrapped up in our local, independent enterprises that the visible, public unity of Christ's faithful church is barely a blip on our radar. Perhaps these words of D. Martyn Lloyd-Jones will challenge us: "Can we deny the charge that we, as evangelical Christians, have been less interested in the question of church unity than anyone else?" He continued, "We are always negative; we are always on the defensive; we are always bringing up objections and difficulties. I do not think we can deny this charge."[23] The problem, I think, is that Calvin was a "big man": the bigger the man (spiritually), the bigger his gospel comprehensiveness, and the bigger his desire to see Christ's "bleeding body" healed of its wounds. There is such a thing as godly ecumenism, and Calvin exhibited it.

A Great Commission Commitment

Fourth, Calvin's commitment to the Great Commission compelled him to pursue reformation beyond Geneva. The church in Geneva was a model for reformation through mission, especially mission to France. Geneva became, wrote Philip Hughes, "the hub of a vast missionary enterprise" and "a dynamic centre or nucleus from which the vital missionary energy it generated radiated out into the world beyond." Under Calvin's oversight and drive, Geneva became a "school of missions" with one supreme aim: "to send out witnesses who would spread the teaching of the Reformation far and wide.... It [Geneva] was a dynamic centre of missionary concern and activity, an axis from which the light of the Good News radiated forth through

22. Ibid., 253.

23. D. Martyn Lloyd-Jones, *Knowing the Times: Addresses Delivered on Various Occasions, 1942–1977* (Edinburgh: Banner of Truth, 1989), 249.

the testimony of those who, after thorough preparation in this school, were sent forth in the service of Jesus Christ,"[24] often to their deaths.

We know for sure that, from 1555 to 1562, eighty-eight preachers were sent from Geneva into France. Of these, nine laid down their lives as martyrs. There may have been more. In 1555, there was only one "dressed church" (i.e. a church constituted and disciplined). Seven years later, in 1562, there were 2,150 such churches! This represents growth of extraordinary proportions. Eventually there were more than two million Protestant church members out of a French population of twenty million. This multiplication came in spite of fierce persecution. For instance, in 1572, seventy thousand Protestants lost their lives. The church order used was Presbyterian. There were twenty-nine national synods from about 1562 to 1685, when persecution forced most of the believers to leave France.

Seeking a Learned Ministry

Fifth, Calvin's drive for a learned and godly ministry ensured that the Reformed faith would be marked by depth as well as by passion. All Calvin's students had to be fully proficient in Latin, Hebrew, and Greek in order to be faithful expositors of God's holy Word—replicating Calvin's own expository ministry. Only when Calvin judged a man "ready" would he be sent into France to preach, plant churches, and die! Was this simply to produce a "well-furnished" ministry? No. With Luther, Calvin could not conceive of any man leading a church who was not spiritually equipped to do so; and part of that necessary spiritual equipment was knowing the languages in which the Holy Spirit's penmen wrote the Holy Scriptures.

Calvin also pursued pedagogical reform through print. Gordon estimates that from 1550 until his death in 1564, Calvin printed upward of one hundred thousand words a year. Also, between 1536 and 1563, approximately 150 Bibles and New Testaments were produced in Geneva.[25] These are astonishing figures. Calvin's massive

24. Philip E. Hughes, "John Calvin: Director of Missions," in *The Heritage of John Calvin,* ed. J. H. Bratt (Grand Rapids: Eerdmans, 1973), 40–54.

25. Gordon, *Calvin,* 288.

output of commentaries, tracts, and treatises gave the Reformation doctrines a biblical, reasoned, and accessible foundation.

Calvin's *Institutes* was perhaps his most enduring pedagogical guide. The work undoubtedly was designed as an introduction to biblical study for theology students. Yet there is a tendency among scholars to draw a false distinction between the pedagogical and devotional purposes in Calvin's writing. For Calvin, true knowledge was nothing less than piety (*pietas*). Thus, at the same time that the *Institutes* provided a grounding in biblical doctrine, it also nourished the souls of multitudes who were thirsting for the true gospel of Christ. In the *Institutes*, men and women encountered the truth of the Bible and discovered Christ, the substance and soul of the gospel.

I have said little about Calvin's letters; no less do they illustrate the breadth and significance of his writing. He wrote letters to kings and princes, to bishops and other clerics, to men in high political office, to pastors facing death, to believers struggling to cope. The real character of Calvin and his drive for reform is revealed in his letter-writing, which was remarkably extensive and pastoral in character, and which was shot through with theological insight. Besides personal letters, he also wrote to the French churches as a whole. One such letter, in November 1559, exposes the heart of Calvin the Reformer: "Persecutions are the true combats of Christians to try the constancy and firmness of their faith.... As for you, my brethren, hold in reverence the blood of the martyrs which is shed for a testimony to the truth, as being dedicated and consecrated to the glory of God."[26] For Calvin, the cause of Christ was worth the life-blood of his faithful people.

Although he himself did not die a martyr's death as such, there is little doubt that Calvin's heart-and-soul commitment to the cause of reformation wore him out. This, for Calvin, was not something to boast about; he felt he had lived as every Christian is to live, "bearing about in the body the death of Jesus, so that the life of Jesus may also be revealed in our body" (2 Cor. 4:10). This is the irreducible minimum of authentic Christian discipleship, or so Calvin believed.

26. Calvin, *Tracts and Letters*, 7:81, 86.

Calvin lived to see the Reformed faith spread throughout Europe and to witness the viciousness of the Counter-Reformation response. He never lived to see the Protestant unity he longed for, but through the massive printing of his works he became what Melanchthon said he was, "the theologian," not of the Reformed faith but of the Protestant faith.

Gordon's conclusion in his very fine biography captures the influence of Calvin the Reformer:

> The extent of Calvin's international influence cannot be measured by confessions, church ordinances or even letters. His works were widely read and his ideas appropriated in varying degrees even in lands that never saw a Reformation. Through personal contacts, his teaching and preaching in Geneva and his correspondence, he reached a vast and diverse body of individuals.... He never attempted to impose his views on church organization, and never regarded Geneva, despite Knox's praise, as the gold standard. Calvin's international work grew from his abiding belief that the visible churches had to be unified in doctrine, not in outward forms. During his life he saw very little of that unity, but through the massive printing of his works he remained in death its most prominent advocate.[27]

---

27. Gordon, *Calvin*, 275.

CHAPTER 3

Calvin's Way of Doing Theology: Exploring the *Institutes*

ANTHONY N. S. LANE

John Calvin is best known for his *Instruction in the Christian Religion* (commonly called the *Institutes*). This work went through five major editions, and Calvin continuously revised it for most of his literary and pastoral life. Like Augustine, he was one of those who write as they learn and learn as they write.[1] In this chapter, I shall start with an account of its development, availability, and purpose before turning to its themes. My aim is to whet your appetite to want to read the *Institutes* for yourself.

Background to the *Institutes*[2]

The first edition of the *Institutes* appeared in 1536, when Calvin was only twenty-six and before he had begun his ministry in Geneva.[3] He probably finished writing it by August 23, 1535, the date of the opening "Prefatory Address." It was published the following March in Basel in a pocket-book format. It was roughly as long as the section

1. John Calvin, *Institutes of the Christian Religion*, ed. John T. McNeill, trans. Ford Lewis Battles, Library of Christian Classics, Vols. 20–21 (London: SCM, and Philadelphia: Westminster Press, 1960), 5 (hereafter, *Inst.*).

2. Material from this and the next three sections will be found in my *Reader's Guide to Calvin's Institutes* (Grand Rapids: Baker, 2009), 16–22. For more on the editions of the *Institutes*, see F. Wendel, *Calvin* (London: Collins, 1963), 111–22, 144–49; R. A. Muller, *The Unaccommodated Calvin* (Oxford: Oxford University Press, 2000), chaps. 6–7.

3. There is an English translation: John Calvin, *Institutes of the Christian Religion*, ed. Ford Lewis Battles (Grand Rapids: Eerdmans and H. H. Meeter Center, 1986 [revised edition]).

of the New Testament from Matthew to Ephesians. There were six chapters. Four covered the law, the creed, the Lord's Prayer and the sacraments (baptism and Lord's Supper)—the traditional components of a catechism. The other two chapters, on the five false (i.e. Roman Catholic) sacraments and on Christian liberty, were more polemical in tone, as was the prefatory address to King Francis I.

The second edition was nearly completed by October 1, 1538, and was published the following August in Strassburg,[4] where Calvin was ministering during his period of exile from Geneva. Although it was published while Calvin was in Strassburg, it was largely written while he was still in Geneva, and those who have suggested the influence of Strassburg and Martin Bucer on this edition have been misled by looking at the date of publication. It was more than twice the length of the first edition, the six chapters having become seventeen. It was a thorough revision of the first edition, and the title page states that "now, at last [it] corresponds to its title."

Calvin made a French translation that appeared in 1541, published in Geneva but aimed at the French market.[5] This was a major event in the history of the French language—the appearance in French of a major theological work. Calvin's elegant French style played an important formative role in the development of French as a modern language. This and later French editions showed Calvin's concern to reach not just the intelligentsia but the laity.

The third edition, a less radical revision, was published in March 1543 at Strassburg. It was nearing completion in January 1542. Thus, while it was completed in Geneva, it reflects the influence of Calvin's three years at Strassburg, which ended in September 1541. The seventeen chapters of 1539 had become twenty-one.

---

4. I have used the German spelling as a reminder that at this stage Strasbourg was still a German city.

5. This has been translated into English by Elsie Anne McKee: John Calvin, *Institutes of the Christian Religion: 1541 French Edition* (Grand Rapids: Eerdmans, 2009).

The fourth edition appeared early in 1550 at Geneva. There was relatively little new material; the main new feature was the division of the chapters into sections for the first time.

During the winter of 1558/9, Calvin lay ill with malaria and determined to produce a definitive edition of the *Institutes.* This appeared in September 1559 at Geneva. In this edition, Calvin added more material and thoroughly rearranged the book. He tells us that while he did not regret the earlier editions, he had not been satisfied with the arrangement until this edition. It is true that he had devoted care to the overall structure of the work, but unfortunately the pressure of work meant that this care did not always extend to the details of the work. We should remember that 2009, as well as being the five-hundredth anniversary of Calvin's birth, is also the 450th anniversary of the definitive edition of the *Institutes.*

This edition is roughly as long as Genesis to Luke, more than five times the length of the first edition. It consists of eighty chapters divided into four books corresponding to the four sections of the Apostles' Creed. Again, Calvin made a French translation, which appeared in 1560. Because this appeared after the final Latin edition, some regard it as the truly definitive version, but that is to mistake the role of the French translations. The Latin is the definitive text, and the translations at times simplify it in order to make it more accessible to non-scholars.

English Translations

There are four English translations of the 1559 *Institutes:*

- The first, by Thomas Norton, Thomas Cranmer's son-in-law, was published in 1561[6] and much reprinted. J. I. Packer has expressed the view that this is the best of the translations,[7] though it is of course in Elizabethan English.

6. John Calvin, *The Institution of Christian Religion* (London: R. Wolffe & R. Harrison, 1561, and many reprints).

7. In a personal conversation.

- The second, by John Allen, was published in 1813.[8] This was a British translation that came to be reprinted especially in the United States, with an introduction by B. B. Warfield on the literary history of the *Institutes.*
- The third, by Henry Beveridge, was published in 1845 as part of the Calvin Translation Society project.[9] This translation is still in print and can sometimes be bought in a single-volume form with very small print. It is also available electronically.[10]
- The fourth, by Ford Lewis Battles, was published in 1960. This is the best version to use because it has the advantage of a superior layout, full notes, and extensive indexes.[11] It also is available electronically.[12]

The Purpose of the *Institutes*

Calvin's aims in preparing the successive editions of the *Institutes* can be discerned by an examination of their title pages and prefaces.

The title page of the 1536 edition is revealing:

> Embracing almost the whole sum of piety and whatever is necessary to know the doctrine of salvation: A work most worthy to be read by all persons zealous for piety.

This edition was meant to be a brief summary of the Christian faith, with the goal of edification. This end was served especially by the first four chapters, which were modelled on the traditional elements of a catechism. But before it appeared, there arose a need for another type of work. In October 1534, a number of "placards"

8. John Calvin, *Institutes of the Christian Religion* (London: P. H. Nicklin, 1813, and many reprints).

9. John Calvin, *Institutes of the Christian Religion* (Edinburgh: Calvin Translation Society, 1845–46, and many reprints).

10. On the CD *John Calvin Collection* (Rio, Wis.: AGES Library, 1998) and online at www.ccel.org.

11. There also have been a number of abridgements of the *Institutes*, such as John Calvin, *The Institutes of Christian Religion*, eds. T. Lane and H. Osborne (London: Hodder & Stoughton, 1986; Grand Rapids: Baker Academic, 1987, and many reprints).

12. On the CD *John Calvin Collection.*

attacking the Roman Mass were posted around Paris—one on the door of the royal bedchamber, if the report is to be believed. The king, Francis I, was furious and launched a vigorous onslaught against the French evangelicals. Francis sought to justify his brutal repression on the grounds that the evangelicals were seditious Anabaptists, which was ground enough for most people at that time. Calvin therefore dedicated the 1536 edition to Francis as a confession of faith *and* as an apology for the French Protestants, as he explains in his "Prefatory Address to the King."[13]

In his "Letter to the Reader" at the beginning of the second edition (1539), Calvin explained how the *Institutes* should be used. It was intended, he said, as an introduction and guide to the study of Scripture, and was designed to complement his commentaries. Because of the *Institutes,* Calvin felt he need not digress at length on doctrinal matters in his commentaries.[14] This warns us against falling into the common error of viewing Calvin as "a man of one book"—the *Institutes.* He devoted much more time to expounding Scripture than to writing the *Institutes.* The *Institutes* and the commentaries were designed to be used together—the *Institutes* to provide a theological undergirding for the commentaries and the latter to provide a more solid exegesis of the passages cited in the former. So when he gave a biblical reference in the *Institutes,* Calvin may have been pointing not just to the biblical text itself, but also to his commentary on that passage.

The French editions from 1541 to 1551 contained an introduction titled "Subject Matter of the Present Work." Here Calvin presented the *Institutes* as a guide to the laity in their study of the Bible. The Scriptures, he explained, contain a perfect doctrine, to which nothing can be added, but the beginner needs guidance in order to study them profitably. The *Institutes* was offered for that purpose, as "a summary of Christian doctrine" and "an introduction to the profitable reading both of the Old and New Testament."

---

13. A helpful account of the 1536 edition is found in T. H. L. Parker, *John Calvin* (London: J. M. Dent, 1975), chap. 3. Calvin also explains why he wrote this edition in his *Commentary on Psalms*, xli–xlii (Author's Preface).

14. Pp. 4–5.

Calvin's *Institutes* is still widely read today, more so than any other major theological work of comparable age. This is partly because of Calvin's great success in his aim of "lucid brevity," of covering a topic briefly while yet expressing clearly what he had to say. That makes his writing easier to read than that of most comparable works. It is also partly because of his great theological skills, which are appreciated even by those who may differ from him on particular doctrines, be that infant baptism or predestination. But we should not lose sight of the fact that this was a book written in the sixteenth century to address sixteenth-century concerns. We can undoubtedly learn much from studying it today, but we must not fall into the trap of imagining that it is addressed to our current situation.

The Structure of the 1559 *Institutes*

For the past century, Calvin scholars have been debating the structure of the 1559 *Institutes*.[15] Calvin gave us his own structure in the titles of the four books:

- Book One: The Knowledge of God the Creator.
- Book Two: The Knowledge of God the Redeemer in Christ...
- Book Three: The Way in Which we Receive the Grace of Christ...
- Book Four: The External Means or Aids by Which God Invites us into the Society of Christ...

Scholars have come up with a number of theories that propose a deeper underlying structure. Edward Dowey claimed, especially on the basis of a comment of Calvin in Book 1, chapter 2, section 1 of the *Institutes*,[16] that the basic structure of the *Institutes* is twofold—the knowledge of God as Creator and as Redeemer.[17] He saw the break

15. See C. Partee, *The Theology of John Calvin* (Louisville: Westminster John Knox, 2008), 35–43.

16. Hereafter, all citations from the *Institutes* will follow the format *Inst.* 1.2.1.

17. E. A. Dowey, *The Knowledge of God in Calvin's Theology* (Grand Rapids: Eerdmans, 1994; revision of 1951 ed.), 41–49.

between these two as coming partway through Book Two.[18] There is this division in the *Institutes*, but to take it as the fundamental division and to divide the *Institutes* in a way that is so different from Calvin's own division is implausible. T. H. L. Parker, more plausibly, argued that the *Institutes* is structured according to the four articles of the Apostles' Creed.[19] This theory has the merit that the contents of each book do roughly match this division—but not exactly. Book 3 would then be about the Holy Spirit, who is not mentioned in Calvin's title. According to this schema, the final resurrection should be addressed in Book Four, whereas it actually is covered at the end of Book Three. So while there are indeed many parallels between the structure of the *Institutes* and that of the Apostles' Creed, if Calvin intended the former to be based on the latter, one can only say that he made a bad job of it.[20] Finally, Charles Partee has proposed a twofold division between "God For Us" (Books One and Two) and "God With Us" (Books Three and Four).[21] It is certainly true that the material fits this twofold division (as it also fits Dowey's twofold division into God as Creator/Redeemer), but that does not mean that Calvin saw either of these as his basic structure. Ultimately, Calvin's own structure is normative, not the underlying structures seen by various scholars.

The Nature of the *Institutes*

Is the *Institutes* a work of systematic theology? In the sense that Calvin worked in an orderly way through the full range of Christian doctrine, yes, it is. But in other important senses, no, it is not. In particular, much systematic theology today seeks to expound the Christian faith

18. Ibid., 45: "Book II really begins only in chapter vi."

19. T. H. L. Parker, *Calvin's Doctrine of the Knowledge of God,* 2nd ed. (Edinburgh: Oliver & Boyd, 1969), 6.

20. The same applies even more to the suggestion of Philip Butin that the Trinity is the organizing or structural paradigm for the 1559 *Institutes*, though he does qualify this by referring to the Apostles' Creed (P. W. Butin, *Revelation, Redemption, and Response: Calvin's Trinitarian Understanding of the Divine-Human Relationship* [New York: Oxford University Press, 1995], 19, 124). A division into four books does not immediately suggest a structure based on the Trinity.

21. Partee, *The Theology of John Calvin*, 40–43.

from the perspective of some controlling principle or axiom. Since the nineteenth century, there have been attempts to read Calvin this way. Some have argued that predestination or the sovereignty of God is a central dogma from which Calvin deduced all of the rest of his teaching. It is generally agreed that such attempts are mistaken, that Calvin did not work that way.

Systematic theologies are usually thought of as cold, logical systems that use philosophical analysis and address the mind. The *Institutes* is very different. Calvin did not avoid all interaction with philosophy, but it is relatively rare. His approach perhaps can best be seen from his definition of faith as "a firm and certain knowledge of God's benevolence toward us, founded upon the truth of the freely given promise in Christ, both revealed to our minds and sealed upon our hearts through the Holy Spirit."[22]

Calvin defines faith as knowledge, but this does not mean that it is confined to the mind. Faith is not to be seen as mere intellectual assent.[23] It is more than accepting the veracity of the Gospel accounts[24] or holding sound doctrine.[25] It is possible to regard the Word of God as an infallible oracle without having saving faith.[26] Assent to facts is important, but faith also includes the personal element. It is not just an opinion or a persuasion but rather a personal confidence in the mercy of God[27] involving not just the mind but also the heart.[28] It

22. *Inst.* 3.2.7.
23. *Inst.* 3.2.8–10, 33.
24. *Inst.* 3.2.1, 9.
25. *Inst.* 3.2.13.
26. *Inst.* 3.2.9–10.
27. *Inst.* 3.2.1, 15–16, 29–30, 43; *Commentary* on Romans 10:10; *Commentary* on Colossians 2:2; *Commentary* on 2 Timothy 1:12; *Commentary* on Hebrews 11:6. R. T. Kendall, *Calvin and English Calvinism to 1649* (Oxford: Oxford University Press, 1979; repr., Carlisle, Pa.: Paternoster, 1997), 19, notes some of the words used by Calvin for faith, including certainty (*certitudino*), firm conviction (*solida persuasio*), firm assurance (*solida securitas*), and full assurance (*plena securitas*) from *Institutes* 3.2.6, 16, 22.
28. *Institutes* 3.2.36; *Commentary* on John 2:23; 5:24; *Commentary* on Acts 16:14; *Commentary* on Hebrews 11:6; *Commentary* on 1 Peter 1:8. Cf. Walter E.

is not sufficient for the mind to be illumined unless the heart is also strengthened and supported, because faith is not just the assent of the mind but also confidence and security of heart. Indeed, the *chief* part of faith is firm and stable constancy of heart.[29] Calvin objected to the Roman idea of faith as mere intellectual assent by pointing out that assent "is more of the heart than of the brain, and more of the disposition than the understanding."[30] Calvin could even state that the seat of faith is not in the brain but in the heart.[31] Faith involves the feelings and affections of the heart, as well as the intellect.[32] It does not just believe the promises of God, but also relies on them, thus bringing confidence and boldness.[33]

Related to this, Calvin states that the gospel "is a doctrine not of the tongue but of life. It is not apprehended by the understanding and memory alone, as other disciplines are, but it is received only when it possesses the whole soul, and finds its seat and resting place in the inmost affection of the heart."[34]

This affected the way in which Calvin wrote the *Institutes*. His style was rhetorical, with the aim not just to inform the intellect but to persuade the whole person. This caused some to misunderstand him. The great Roman Catholic polemicist Robert Bellarmine, writing a generation later, accused Calvin of being inaccurate because he indulged in hyperbole or exaggeration, not realizing that Calvin's humanist style was very different from his (Bellarmine's) precise scholastic style.[35]

Stuermann, *A Critical Study of Calvin's Concept of Faith* (Tulsa, Okla.: University of Tulsa Press, 1952), 87–102, where faith is analyzed as the experience of certainty, the illumination of the mind, and the sealing of the heart.

29. *Inst.* 3.2.33.

30. *Inst.* 3.2.8.

31. *Commentary* on Romans 10:10; cf. *Inst.* 1.5.9; 3.2.36.

32. *Inst.* 3.2.8; *Commentary* on Matthew 11:12; *Commentary* on John 2:23; *Commentary* on Acts 16:14; *Commentary* on Romans 10:10; *Commentary* on Philippians 3:10.

33. *Commentary* on Ephesians 3:12; cf. *Inst.* 3.2.36.

34. *Inst.* 3.6.4.

35. R. W. Richgels, "Scholasticism Meets Humanism in the Counter-Reformation: The Clash of Cultures in Robert Bellarmine's Use of Calvin in the *Controversies*," *Sixteenth Century Journal* 6 (1975): 53–66.

THE TEACHING OF THE *INSTITUTES*

In the remainder of this chapter, I shall examine a number of the doctrines taught in the *Institutes*, with the aim of whetting your appetite to turn to it and read it for yourself.

Predestination

When people ask, "Are you a Calvinist?" they usually mean, "Do you believe in a particular doctrine of predestination?" This is an unfortunate meaning of the question, for a number of reasons. First, predestination was just one doctrine for Calvin, not the central doctrine or the most important one. Second, predestination was not Calvin's most distinctive doctrine. On this matter he largely followed Martin Luther and Ulrich Zwingli, who in turn stood in a medieval tradition. Belief in predestination was almost universal among the sixteenth-century Reformers, though it is true that Calvin's doctrine went further than some people's. Third, the question often means, "Do you hold to the Five Points of Calvinism, as summarized in the mnemonic TULIP?" (TULIP stands for *t*otal depravity, *u*nconditional election, *l*imited atonement, *i*rresistible grace, and *p*erseverance of the saints.) Far from going back to Calvin, this particular formulation (TULIP) probably originated in the 1920s![36] (Of course, the doctrines referred to by the five letters go back much further.) Also, many scholars maintain that Calvin himself did not hold to the third point (limited atonement), though others disagree.

So let us examine some of the other doctrines found in the *Institutes*, looking especially at areas where (unlike predestination) Calvin's teaching was distinctive.

---

36. K. J. Stewart, "The Points of Calvinism: Retrospect and Prospect," *Scottish Bulletin of Evangelical Theology* 26 (2008): 187–203.

The Inner Witness of the Spirit[37]

Calvin asks, of the Bible, "Who can convince us that these writings came from God?"[38] Faced with our own doubts and the attacks of sceptics, how can we be sure that the Bible is the Word of God with the certainty of faith? Here is an issue that is, if anything, *more* relevant today than it was in Calvin's time. So how did he answer?

Calvin considered two possible answers, each of which has value but is insufficient in itself. One answer is that we know that the Bible is the Word of God because the church tells us. Calvin was wary of this argument because of where it could lead. If you accept the Bible only because the church tells you, why do you not also accept the church's interpretation of Scripture? Calvin did not deny that the church has a role in commending Scripture (how could he?), but he said this does not suffice. "What will happen to miserable consciences seeking firm assurance of eternal life if all the promises of it consist in and depend solely upon the judgment of men?"[39] Incidentally, Calvin was concerned about Scripture not primarily as a textbook from which to build an intellectual system but as the basis for assurance before God, as a basis for Christian living.

Another possible answer is to base our belief in Scripture as God's Word on rational apologetic arguments. Calvin did not deny that there is a place for this and devoted the next chapter of the *Institutes* to presenting just such a case.[40] But he made it clear that rational arguments are inadequate, that at best they produce a probable opinion, not the certainty of faith.[41] It is also noteworthy that Calvin's apologetic arguments in this chapter are more dated than almost anything else in the *Institutes* and are of little value today.

So on what should we primarily base our confidence in Scripture? "The highest proof of Scripture derives in general from the fact that

---

37. More relating to this section will be found in my "John Calvin: The Witness of the Holy Spirit," in *Faith and Ferment* (Westminster Conference, 1982): 1–6.

38. *Inst.* 1.7.1.

39. Ibid.

40. *Inst.* 1.8.

41. *Inst.* 1.7.4.

God in person speaks in it."[42] The Holy Spirit bears witness to us that the Scriptures are God's Word. "The same Spirit, therefore, who has spoken through the mouths of the prophets must penetrate into our hearts to persuade us that they faithfully proclaimed what had been divinely commanded."[43]

What was Calvin referring to? Was he saying that when we visit the religious section of a bookshop and look at the scriptures of different religions, when we reach the Bible the Spirit whispers in our ears and says, "That's the one"? No. Rather, the Holy Spirit opens our eyes so that we can see what is there, what is self-evident for those with eyes to see. "Scripture exhibits fully as clear evidence of its own truth as white and black things do of their color, or sweet and bitter things do of their taste."[44] Also, this is not some esoteric experience given to a few: "I speak of nothing other than what each believer experiences within himself."[45] Calvin urged believers to accept the Bible because of the way God speaks to them through it. Once that is established, there is a role for the witness of the church to confirm it and for apologetic arguments, but as a "secondary aid."[46]

Faith and Assurance[47]

There are strands of the Reformed, Calvinist tradition for which assurance has become a problem. This is especially acute among some circles that claim assurance of salvation is almost seen as presumptuous. An illustration is used that a sheep has a mark of ownership on its ear that can be seen by all—except by the sheep itself. The message is clear. If you are a Christian, it should be plain to everyone—except yourself. In those circles, there is a tradition of people noted for their great sanctity refraining from actually claiming to be converted.

42. Ibid.

43. Ibid.

44. *Inst.* 1.7.2.

45. *Inst.* 1.7.5.

46. *Inst.* 1.8.1, 13.

47. More relating to this section will be found in my "Calvin's Doctrine of Assurance Revisited," forthcoming in *Tributes to John Calvin: A Celebration of His Quincentenary*, ed. David W. Hall (Phillipsburg, N.J.: P&R, 2010).

Indeed, reluctance to claim this is itself at times seen as evidence of sanctification.

Allied to this is the myth that Calvin denied that we can know whether we are elect and that he himself died in despair. Both of these are totally untrue. There is no shortage of evidence about his last days, and he clearly died confident of salvation. Again, so far was he from teaching that it is impossible to have assurance of salvation that he actually held that assurance of salvation is itself part of saving faith. (In doing so, he was following in the steps of Luther, Philip Melanchthon, and other mainstream Reformers.) This followed from his definition of faith, already quoted: "a firm and certain knowledge of God's benevolence toward us, founded upon the truth of the freely given promise in Christ, both revealed to our minds and sealed upon our hearts through the Holy Spirit."[48]

If saving faith is a knowledge of God's benevolence that extends to the heart as well as the head, it makes no sense for someone to have that heart confidence but not be confident of God's forgiveness:

> Briefly, he alone is truly a believer who, convinced by a firm conviction that God is a kindly, and well-disposed Father *toward him*, promises himself all things on the basis of his generosity; who, relying upon the promises of divine benevolence toward him, lays hold on an undoubted expectation of salvation.[49]

On its own, this statement would be pastorally very insensitive. It would mean that anyone who doubted the fact of his or her salvation would prove by so doing that he or she was not saved. But Calvin was fully aware that genuine believers can and do have doubts:

> Surely, while we teach that faith ought to be certain and assured, we cannot imagine any certainty that is not tinged with doubt, or any assurance that is not assailed by some anxiety. On the other hand, we say that believers are in perpetual conflict with their own unbelief. Far, indeed, are we from putting their consciences in any peaceful repose, undisturbed by any tumult at all.[50]

48. *Inst.* 3.2.7.
49. *Inst.* 3.2.16.
50. *Inst.* 3.2.17.

Isn't this hopelessly confused? No. On the one hand, Calvin insisted that saving faith is not just a belief that God is favorable to some people, we know not whom—the Roman Catholic view. Faith is a trust in God's promises of salvation that, almost by definition, implies some degree of assurance of salvation. But all believers, to a greater or lesser extent, struggle against doubt. These doubts can undermine our assurance of salvation. But the cure for this is not to seek assurance as something totally separate from faith, but rather to strengthen our faith and thereby our assurance.

The difference on this point between Calvin and some others in the Reformed tradition relates to the question of the ultimate ground for assurance. For Calvin, it is not predestination, good works, experience of the Holy Spirit, or even our faith, but simply Christ and the promises of the gospel. These other things all have a role to play in assurance, but not as the ultimate ground. It is the same as with the inner witness of the Spirit to Scripture, where the church and rational arguments can play a subsidiary role. Seeing the evidence of good works in our lives can strengthen our assurance, but if we rely primarily on that in order to know that we are indeed children of God, we will have trouble. We are liable either to fall into a false self-confidence or to lapse into despair. As Calvin put it, "newness of life, as the effect of divine adoption, serves to confirm confidence; but as a secondary support, whereas we must be founded on grace alone."[51]

The Christian Life

Five chapters of the *Institutes* are devoted to the Christian life, clear evidence that Calvin's aim was not just to inform the mind but to move the heart through the mind. These chapters bear the clear imprint of the medieval *Devotio Moderna*, as exemplified especially by Thomas à Kempis's so-called *Imitation of Christ*, but translated from a medieval monastic to a Protestant "secular" setting of those living "in the world."

51. *Commentary* on 1 John 4:17.

The first three chapters cover the imitation of Christ (3:6), self-denial (3:7), and bearing our crosses (3:8). A key verse underlying Calvin's teaching here would be Matthew 16:24: "If anyone will come after me, let him deny himself, and take up his cross, and follow me." This goes to the heart of discipleship and what it costs.

The last two chapters (3:9–10) concern the correct attitude to this world and the next. Here, as well as in the earlier chapters, Calvin sets out general principles that help us to deal with one of the pressing issues we face today—that of simplicity of lifestyle. There are two dangers that Christians face, especially those who live in the West. The first is an affluent materialism that runs counter to the teaching of the gospels. The second is a legalism that seeks to tell Christians what they may or may not have. Such an approach can soon become dated—such as the teaching at one stage that it is acceptable for Christians to have black-and-white TVs, but not color TVs.

How can we combat the materialism without lapsing into legalism? Calvin sets out some general principles that, in my view, translate well into other cultures and can be applied in twenty-first century London as well as sixteenth-century Geneva. We are to be detached from the things of this world to the extent that we recognize that this is not our permanent home. In themselves, they are good gifts of God and are to be accepted as such, but *in comparison with* our future goal, they are to be despised as worthless. This view does not encourage asceticism. These are God's gifts and there is no virtue in rejecting them. But meditation on our future life relativizes them and warns us against becoming enslaved to them, against making idols of them. They are to be used so far as they help us on our way.

They are to be used, but there is a need for moderation. On the one hand, we are to avoid a legalistic asceticism. There is nothing wrong with enjoyment per se, and food is given to us to enjoy as well as to keep us alive. On the other hand, we should be frugal and avoid all excess, whether gluttony, drunkenness, or whatever. All that we have from God is given in trust for us to use for His glory. We also are called to be generous to those in need. Generosity is not a legal category. It is not about paying a certain percentage, as if we were paying taxes.

Furthermore, generosity implies giving with compassion, not the cold charity that treats its objects with contempt.

Justification by Faith[52]

Calvin is a leading exponent of the Protestant doctrine of justification by faith, which I will summarize briefly before turning to a little-noted oddity in his teaching. Calvin understood justification in forensic terms. To be justified is to be accepted by God as righteous, to be declared righteous, to be acquitted. Justification is a "not guilty" verdict in a law court. Calvin defined it as "the acceptance with which God receives us into his favor as righteous men" and added that "it consists in the remission of sins and the imputation of Christ's righteousness."[53]

Related to this definition of justification is his distinction between justification and sanctification or regeneration. These two must be distinguished, he said, but cannot be separated. Justification and sanctification are like the two legs of a pair of trousers, not like a pair of socks, which may well become separated and, in my experience, too often do.

How are we justified? Justification is in Christ alone and by Christ alone. "We are reckoned righteous before God in Christ and apart from ourselves."[54] Justification is also by faith alone, but faith is of value not as a virtue in its own right but as faith *in Christ*. "We say that faith justifies, not because it merits righteousness for us by its own worth, but because it is an instrument whereby we obtain freely the righteousness of Christ."[55] Calvin compared faith to an empty vessel with which we come to receive Christ's grace. The power of justification lies not in faith itself, but in the Christ who is received by faith.[56]

---

52. More relating to this section will be found in my "The Role of Scripture in Calvin's Doctrine of Justification," in *John Calvin and the Interpretation of Scripture: Calvin Studies 10 & 11,* ed. C. Raynal (Grand Rapids: Calvin Studies Society, 2006), 368–84.

53. *Inst.* 3.11.2.

54. *Inst.* 3.11.4.

55. *Inst.* 3.18.8.

56. *Inst.* 3.11.7.

Central to Calvin's doctrine of salvation is the concept of union with Christ.[57] This is seen most clearly from the structure of his *Institutes*. Having expounded his doctrine of the person of Christ and what He achieved for us in Book Two, in Book Three he turns to "The Way in which we Receive the Grace of Christ."[58] There he starts by affirming that "as long as Christ remains outside of us, and we are separated from him, all that he has suffered and done for the salvation of the human race remains useless and of no value for us."[59] Until we are united with Christ, what He has achieved for us helps us no more than an electrical main that passes a house but is not connected to it. The Holy Spirit unites us with Christ, by faith, which brings us two major benefits—justification and sanctification. "Now, both repentance and forgiveness of sins—that is, newness of life and free reconciliation—are conferred on us by Christ, and both are attained by us through faith."[60] These benefits are the theme of most of the remainder of Book Three.

In order to make it clear that we cannot have justification without sanctification, Calvin first devotes eight chapters to the latter[61] before turning to the former,[62] making it clear that forgiveness of sins cannot be separated from holiness of life. Justification and sanctification are inseparable because they both flow from union with Christ, which Calvin once (and only once) describes as a "mystical union."[63] "As Christ cannot be torn into parts, so these two which we perceive in him together and conjointly are inseparable—namely, righteousness and sanctification. Whomever, therefore, God receives into grace, on

57. For two recent studies on union with Christ in Calvin, see J. T. Billings, *Calvin, Participation, and the Gift: The Activity of Believers in Union with Christ* (Oxford: Oxford University Press, 2007); Mark A. Garcia, *Life in Christ: Union with Christ and Twofold Grace in Calvin's Theology* (Carlisle, U.K.: Paternoster, 2008).

58. *Inst.* 3.title.

59. *Inst.* 3.1.1.

60. *Inst.* 3.3.1.

61. *Inst.* 3.3–10.

62. *Inst.* 3.11–19.

63. *Inst.* 3.11.10.

them he at the same time bestows the Spirit of adoption, by whose power he remakes them to his own image."[64]

So faith unites us with Christ, and it is "in him" that we are justified and have new life. Justification is not a benefit that Christ confers on us, which we then possess independently of Him. We are justified only by virtue of being in Christ. For Calvin, justification and sanctification both follow inevitably from union with Christ. He appeals to 1 Corinthians 1:30 to show that Christ is given to us for both righteousness and sanctification. "Therefore Christ justifies no one whom he does not at the same time sanctify."[65] It should be noted that Calvin, unlike some of his interpreters, does not speak of justification as the cause of sanctification nor of the latter as the fruit or consequence of the former. Both are the fruit and consequence of union with Christ.[66] Perhaps the confusion arises in part because justification is complete from the beginning, while sanctification is progressive. Thus, the event of justification is followed by the process of sanctification. But it would be wrong to deduce that, for Calvin, the latter is the *consequence* of the former.

Calvin was keen to exclude human works from justification. He argues that the Pharisee in the parable (Luke 18:9–14) trusted in the merit of his works only because he was judging them by the wrong standard. When we see God's holiness, His justice, His law, His standards, and His requirements, our response can only be that of the tax collector, to cast ourselves on God's mercy alone with trembling and humility. This involves a real humility, not just a feigned, polite modesty. It is not to be confused with the schoolboy definition of humility as pretending to be what you know you are not. This is nothing

64. *Inst.* 3.11.6.

65. *Inst.* 3.16.1.

66. Luther tended to see sanctification as the fruit of justification rather than seeing them both as flowing from union with Christ. Cf. Jonathan Rainbow, "Double Grace: John Calvin's View of the Relationship of Justification and Sanctification," *Ex Auditu,* 5 (1989): 102–103. Calvin often affirmed that justification and regeneration/sanctification are distinct without being separated (e.g. *Inst.* 3.11.11).

less than a sober appraisal of the reality of the situation.[67] For Calvin, as he explains at the beginning of his *Institutes*, the knowledge of God and the knowledge of ourselves are intimately related to one another. It is only as we come to an awareness of God's majesty and holiness that we begin to appreciate our sinful state. This was the experience of those in both Testaments who felt the presence of God.[68]

If this were all Calvin had to say, it could be viewed as a negatively depressing and demotivating message. What is the point of bothering to do good? Why seek to serve God if one's best works will be flung back in one's face as tainted and inadequate? As believers, however, we relate to God not as a strict Judge through the law but as our gracious Father through Christ. This leads to Calvin's doctrine of "double justification."

When we approach God in faith, we are accepted as righteous in Christ. But it is not only we who are accepted. God also accepts our good works in Christ, overlooking whatever defects and impurities may remain in them. "Therefore, as we ourselves, when we have been engrafted in Christ, are righteous in God's sight because our iniquities are covered by Christ's sinlessness, so our works are righteous and are thus regarded because whatever fault is otherwise in them is buried in Christ's purity, and is not charged to our account." Thus, "by faith alone not only we ourselves but our works as well are justified."[69]

Finally, I would like to draw attention to a little-noticed oddity in Calvin's teaching on this point, a passage where he appears to teach justification by works. Calvin goes to great pains to deny any inherent value or merit to our works. God accepts these works—but only in Christ and purely of His great generosity. Given that these works are in themselves worthless, it may at first seem surprising that Calvin has a doctrine of justification by these worthless works. That is, he *once* states that we are also accepted by God on the basis of these works. This comes where Calvin is wrestling with the case of Cornelius, about

67. *Inst.* 3.12.1–8.

68. *Inst.* 1.1.1–3.

69. *Inst.* 3.17.10.

whom Peter states that all who act righteously are acceptable to God.[70] This passage can be reconciled with others only if we acknowledge "a double acceptance of man before God."[71] The first is, of course, being accepted in Christ by faith. Thereafter, God also accepts believers as a "new creation" (2 Cor. 5:17) in respect of their works. This is possible for two reasons. First, as we have seen, God chooses to give this value to them. Second, He Himself is the author of this righteousness. "For the Lord cannot fail to love and embrace the good things that he works in them through his Spirit," and so, in Christ, and by grace, "God 'accepts' believers by reason of works."[72] Calvin shortly after argues that because God graciously accepts our works in Christ, "we shall concede not only a partial righteousness in works, as our adversaries themselves hold, but also that it is approved by God as if it were whole and perfect."[73]

Calvin does not say in so many words that believers are also "justified by their works," but acceptance "by reason of works" can mean nothing else. As so often in Calvin, some of the most interesting features in his theology appear where he is forced by his reading of Scripture or of Augustine, or the arguments of his opponents, to make concessions that he otherwise would have been most unlikely to have made.

After his statement about "double acceptance," Calvin proceeds to explain the idea of acceptance on the basis of works by expounding his doctrine of double justification, of the acceptance of our good works on the basis of faith.[74] He then proceeds to discuss James's teaching and its relation to Paul's.[75] Here, of course, he has to handle James's statement that we are justified by works and not by faith alone (2:24). This he expounds differently from Acts 10. For James, "justification" refers to "the declaration, not the imputation, of righteousness.... He is not discussing in what manner we are justified but demanding

---

70. *Inst.* 3.17.4–5.
71. *Inst.* 3.17.4.
72. *Inst.* 3.17.5.
73. *Inst.* 3.17.10.
74. *Inst.* 3.17.8–10.
75. *Inst.* 3.17.11–12.

of believers a righteousness fruitful in good works."[76] While Calvin interprets Acts 10 as an example of a double acceptance by God, he sees James 2 as teaching not acceptance by God but the proof of the genuineness of Abraham's faith.

Why does he treat these passages so differently and introduce these ideas? I think the answer lies not in any systematic considerations but in the fact that Calvin was above all a careful exegete who interpreted each passage according to what it actually says. In other words, the reason lies, I would suggest, in Calvin's commitment to Scripture. Unlike some systematic theologians today, he was committed to listening to and accommodating even those passages that did not easily fit into his theology. Of course, he did not always succeed in achieving this, but it was his conscientious aim. The fact is abundantly clear that many passages of Scripture do teach that "the good works of believers are reasons why the Lord benefits them."[77] Calvin felt obliged to accommodate such passages within his theology—and had he felt inclined not to do so, there was no shortage of Roman Catholic polemicists eager to advertize the fact.

The Lord's Supper[78]

If there was one doctrine that divided Protestants in the early years of the Reformation, it was the presence of Christ in the Lord's Supper. Luther rejected the Roman doctrine of transubstantiation but held tenaciously to a belief in the real presence of Christ. He held that the body and blood of Christ are to be found "in, with and under" the bread and wine—much as water is to be found in a wet sponge. So everyone who eats the bread, whether believer or unbeliever, worthy or unworthy, also eats Christ's body—the former to their salvation, the latter to their condemnation. Zwingli, the Reformer of Zurich, moved to a position that saw the bread and wine just as symbols to remind us

76. *Inst.* 3.17.12.

77. *Inst.* 3.14.21.

78. More relating to this section will be found in my "Was Calvin a Crypto-Zwinglian?" in *Adaptations of Calvinism in Reformation Europe: Essays in Honour of Brian G. Armstrong,* ed. Mack P. Holt (Aldershot, U.K.: Ashgate, 2007), 21–41.

of Christ. They met at the Colloquy of Marburg in October 1529, but famously failed to reach any agreement.

Bucer came to Marburg as a Lutheran but came to the conclusion that a middle way was possible. This he developed and taught. Calvin broadly followed Bucer, and their view remains today a third Protestant option between those of Luther and Zwingli.

Calvin agreed with Zwingli that since Christ's body is human, it cannot be in two places at the same time. His ascended body is seated in the heavenlies, so it cannot be present on earth. In particular, there can be no local or bodily presence of His body in, with, or under the bread. It follows that we don't feed on Christ orally (through the mouth) and therefore that unbelievers do not receive Christ's body. But this measure of agreement did not make Calvin a Zwinglian. He agreed that the bread and wine are symbols, but affirmed that they are not lying or deceitful symbols. This means that the reality signified (Christ's body and blood) is truly exhibited and offered. The Lord's Supper can be compared to a check, which needs to be cashed by faith. But what is the cash value? Through faith, we feed on the body and blood of Christ, entering into a real communion with His flesh.

So for Calvin, Christ's body and blood are offered to all, but received only inwardly by faith. This view is well summarized by the exhortation in the Anglican Book of Common Prayer: "Feed on him in thy heart by faith with thanksgiving." But how is this possible? How can Calvin say with Zwingli that Christ's body and blood are located in heaven and with Luther that we feed upon them? Here, as often in his theology, the Holy Spirit provides the key. It is not that Christ literally descends to earth or we literally ascend to heaven. It is the Spirit who unites us with Christ's body and blood in heaven and feeds us with them, giving us communion with them. Calvin used the helpful analogy of the sun. The sun remains some 93 million miles from us, but if you lie out under it on a hot summer's day, you will have a real communion with it—through the medium of the sun's rays. The sun does not descend to earth, but we do a lot more than just remember it.

From the beginning, some Lutherans maintained that Calvin was teaching a subtle form of Zwinglianism, wrapped up in Lutheran language of feeding on Christ's body. On the one hand, this charge is not altogether fair to Calvin. His doctrine breathes a different spirit than Zwingli's. But on the other hand, his doctrine is not as clearly removed from Zwingli's as he liked to suppose and, in my judgment, the charge is not without some validity. An interesting development in recent years has been the interest shown in Calvin's doctrine by a number of Roman Catholics, both scholars and churchmen, who find his approach more acceptable than the official teaching of their church.

Conclusion

These are just a few of the topics covered in Calvin's *Institutes*. I hope that this brief taste may have whetted your appetite to look at the work for yourself.

II. Doctrine and Experience

CHAPTER 4

Calvin and Union with Christ: The Heart of Christian Doctrine

Paul Wells

Abraham Kuyper cautioned those who tackle the subject of union with Christ in John Calvin's theology: "Although Calvin may have been the most rigid among the reformers, yet not one of them has presented this *unio mystica*, this spiritual union with Christ, so incessantly, so tenderly and with such holy fire as he."[1] Any description of Calvin's thought surely will not equal the brio of the maestro!

Apart from the complexity of Calvin's work, particularly concerning how this subject relates to the Lord's Supper, two other attendant difficulties arise with regard to the present theological debate. On the one hand, discussions about the structure of the *Institutes of the Christian Religion*, à la Richard Muller,[2] have tended to make union with Christ a focus in the whole of Calvin's theology. On the other, by way of implication, union with Christ is seen as the motivational force behind the double grace of justification and sanctification, and the objective and subjective aspects of faith, raising anew questions as to the forensic character of justification in the Reformer's thought.[3]

One might be tempted simply to engage with what others have said in recent publications that present the ongoing debate. When

1. Abraham Kuyper, *The Work of the Holy Spirit* (New York: Funk and Wagnalls, 1900), 324–45.

2. See Richard A. Muller, *The Unaccommodated Calvin* (Oxford: Oxford University Press, 2000), 137–39.

3. Issues explored in Richard B. Gaffin, "Justification and Union with Christ," in *A Theological Guide to Calvin's Institutes*, ed. David W. Hall and Peter A. Lillback (Phillipsburg, N.J.: P&R, 2008), chap. 11.

this happens, Calvin's writing itself becomes a pretext for academic jousting. I will try to avoid this by examining three specific biblical texts after some introductory remarks.

Center and Movement in Calvin's Theology

The remarks that follow do not pretend to make a new contribution to the debate regarding the center of Calvin's theology or to interact with what others say on the subject. They seek simply to present a model I have found useful for understanding the relation of three *conexi* in his thought. Whereas the idea of "center" implies something static, Calvin's thought patterns involve a movement characteristic of the development of redemptive history.

I suggest that union with Christ does in fact constitute a central focus of Calvin's theology as a whole, and it does so because it is the resolution of two dialectical tensions that precede and contextualize it: the Creator-creature tension and the more specific divine-human tension.[4] In its turn, it issues in two dialectical situations that are outcomes of the central union with Christ: the dialectical situation of Christ uniting Himself to the believer for the believer's union to Him, and the situation of the believer justified and sanctified. From the original situation to the ultimate resolution, there is a movement in the story involving God and man.

Fundamental to Calvin's work is a dialectic between Creator and creature that structures the whole. As François Wendel states:

> Calvin places all his theology under the sign of what was one of the essential principles of the Reform: the absolute transcendence of God and his total "otherness" in relation to man. No theology is Christian and in conformity with the Scriptures but in the degree to which it respects the infinite distance separating God from his creature and gives up all confusion, all "mixing" that might tend to efface the radical distinction between the Divine

4. These terms are used in a general sense and not to interact with any ongoing academic debate on the subject, such as the work of Brian G. Armstrong and others discussed in Mark A. Garcia's book *Life in Christ: Union with Christ and Twofold Grace in Calvin's Theology* (Carlisle: Paternoster, 2008), 21ff.

> and the human. Above all, God and man must again be seen in their rightful places. That is the idea that dominates the whole of Calvin's theological exposition, and underlies the majority of his controversies.[5]

Quite apart from any consideration of man's fallen nature, there is an irreducible space that constitutes an insurmountable barrier to any imagined contiguity between God and man.[6] Man is radically subordinate to God, and theology can never forget the reality of this situation.[7] Creation, the covenant, redemption, and eschatology, together with their specific orders, express the difference between God and all else, and institutionalize the primacy of God. It is into the distance between the transcendent God in His "otherness" and His creatures that mediation is introduced as a *sine qua non* for contact between them. This fundamental dialectic provides the context for the necessity of mediation and Christ as Mediator, not only in the incarnation but also with a much broader perspective.[8]

The second dialectic resolved by union with Christ is the more specific dialectic of God and humanity.[9] The position and act of mediation assumed by Christ is focused in His work as it relates to God and man, and also as it involves the person of Christ Himself. Mediation finds expression in incarnation, particularly in the fact that the Mediator was not only true man but also true God, the traditional Chalcedonian theological motif. In the person of Christ, there is no "mixing" of the divine and human natures. Both natures exist in the one person, yet without any fusion of the divine and human. The

---

5. François Wendel, *Calvin: The Origins and Development of His Religious Thought,* trans. Philip Mairet (London: William Collins, 1965), 151.

6. Cf. Pierre Gisel, *Le Christ de Calvin* (Paris: Desclée, 1990).

7. Alexandre Ganoczy, *Calvin, théologien de l'Eglise et du ministère* (Paris: Editions du Cerf, 1964), 75.

8. Hendrik Schroten, *Christus, de Middelaar bij Calvijn* (Utrecht: P. den Boer, 1948).

9. On the mediation of Christ, see my article, "The Work of Christ," in *For A New Reformation: Celebrating the Life and Teaching of John Calvin,* ed. Derek W. H. Thomas and John Tweeddale, forthcoming from Crossway.

dialectic of human and divine nature is resolved by the union of humanity and divinity within Christ Himself, and by His work.

It is Christ's work as the incarnate Mediator that is then applied to the believer. Thus, Chapter 12 of Calvin's *Institutes*, on the incarnation, is central in Book Two, which is itself the gate to Book Three on the application of redemption.[10] Christ's humanity draws God closer to us, revealing love and compassion, and providing us with a concrete pledge of salvation. As Calvin says:

> Relying on this pledge, we trust that we are sons of God, for God's natural Son fashioned for himself a body from our body, flesh from our flesh, bones from our bones that he might be one with us.... He took our nature upon himself to impart to us what was his, and to become both Son of God and Son of man in common with us.[11]

We might say that Christ united Himself to us in order to unite us to Himself, and that union with Christ is the outcome of mediation. This is the first dialectical situation that results from the mediation of Christ: His union with us for our union with Him. Christ, as Calvin says, did not receive gifts and graces from God for Himself, but for us:

> As long as Christ remains outside of us, and we are separated from him, all that he has suffered and done for the salvation of the human race remains useless and of no value for us. Therefore, to share with us what he has received from the Father, he had to become ours and to dwell within us. For this reason, he is called "our Head" (Ep 4.15) and "the firstborn among many brethren" (Ro 8.29). We also, in turn are said to be "engrafted into him" (Ro 11.17) and to "put on Christ" (Ga 3.27); for all that he possesses is nothing to us until we grow into one body with him. It is true that we obtain this by faith. Yet since we see that not all indiscriminately embrace that communion with Christ, which

---

10. Calvin argued that both natures were involved in the act of mediation. Cf. Stephen Edmondson, *Calvin's Christology* (Cambridge: Cambridge University Press, 2004), chap. 1.

11. John Calvin, *Institutes of the Christian Religion*, ed. John T. McNeill, trans. Ford Lewis Battles (Philadelphia: Westminster Press, 1960), Book 2, chapter 12, section 2. Hereafter the format *Inst.* 2.12.2 will be used.

> is offered through the gospel, reason itself teaches us to climb higher and to examine into the secret energy of the Spirit, by which we come to enjoy Christ and all his benefits.[12]

Union with Christ is therefore the only way by which believers can receive the goodness that flows through Christ. It is evident from this that the Christ in question here is the living Christ, and that we obtain His blessings by faith through the secret work of the Spirit. Union with Christ is therefore a living relationship of faith and trust that issues from Christ as the source and through the work of the Holy Spirit. Further on in Book Three, refuting Andreas Osiander's notion of essential grace, Calvin states:

> We are deprived of this utterly incomparable good until Christ is made ours. Therefore, that joining together of Head and members, that indwelling of Christ in our hearts—in short, that mystical union—are accorded by us the highest degree of importance, so that Christ, having been made ours, makes us sharers with him in the gifts with which he has been endowed. We do not, therefore, contemplate him outside ourselves from afar in order that his righteousness may be imputed to us but because we put on Christ and are engrafted into his body—in short, because he deigns to make us one with him.[13]

Because we are made one with Christ and joined to Him, there accrues to us the twofold grace expressed in a triangular relationship. This is the second dialectical situation resulting from the mediation of Christ: we are at once definitively justified and progressively sanctified. Partaking in Christ has precedence over the graces of justification and sanctification that flow from Him.[14] As Calvin says in a classic passage:

> By partaking in him, we principally receive a double grace: namely, that being reconciled to God through Christ's blamelessness, we may have instead of a Judge a gracious Father; and secondly, that

12. *Inst.* 3.1.1. Cf. *Commentary* on John 15:1.

13. *Inst.* 3.11.10.

14. Gaffin, "Justification and Union with Christ," 268–69.

> sanctified by Christ's Spirit we may cultivate blamelessness and purity of life.[15]

The structure is plain: first, participation in Him; then the consequence of union, reconciliation with God, who is no longer a Judge, a sort of longhand for justification; then sanctification by the indwelling Spirit. Here we have, based on union with Christ, a reality in the life of the believer that reproduces the image of mediation with its divine and human aspects in the one person of Christ. Justification represents the divine forensic aspect of grace, the truth that God is no longer a Judge but a Father—grace outside of us and for us. Sanctification, an inner transformation, is the fruit of grace in us, renewing our human nature. As in the union of the divine and human natures in the one person of Jesus, Christ is not riven apart or divided when we are joined with Him,[16] but we receive the grace of the whole Christ in justification and holiness of life. This is effected through the work of the Holy Spirit and the instrumentality of faith.[17]

As the instrument of justification and sanctification, the Holy Spirit replicates what Christ does in the mediation of the incarnation. The Holy Spirit is the bond that unites us to Christ effectively. Wendel comments:

> One may justifiably wonder whether the Holy Spirit does not occupy a position, in our relations with the Christ, analogous to that of the Christ himself in his relations with the Father. In a good many passages, indeed, the Holy Spirit plays the part of an

15. *Inst.* 3.11.1. Calvin goes on to explain why he has spoken in this section about sanctification before dealing with justification.

16. *Commentary* on Romans 6:1: "Those who imagine that gratuitous righteousness is given to us by Christ, apart from newness of life, shamefully rend Christ asunder."

17. Cf. J. Todd Billings, *Calvin, Participation, and the Gift* (Oxford: Oxford University Press, 2008), 106–108. The graces are "distinct but inseparable. There is no temporal gap between the two graces." On the forensic aspect, Billings says that Calvin insists upon "a theology of participation involving a forensic act of divine pardon. Through receiving God's forgiveness by Christ's work on the cross, believers participate in the righteousness of Christ which is beyond ourselves" (66). Cf. Gaffin, "Justification and Union with Christ," 253–56.

> obligatory mediator between Christ and man, just as the Christ is the mediator between God and man. And in the same way that Jesus Christ is the necessary instrument of redemption, so is the Holy Spirit the no less necessary instrument by means of which this redemption reaches us, in justification and regeneration.[18]

In the application of salvation, the twofold grace has a precise structure. It shows that, through the work of the Holy Spirit, faith unites to Christ in justification and sanctification as two different but complementary aspects of union with Christ.

The Creator-creature and divine-human dialectics are thus resolved by the mediation of Christ. The mediation brings about union with Christ in the accomplishment of redemption, and the application of redemption through the double grace, and finally has its goal in the end of redemption, when God will be "all in all." Christ at this future point will deliver "the kingdom to God the Father" (1 Cor. 15:24, 28). In a sense, the dialectics are transcended, as also is mediatorship, when we "enjoy the direct vision of the Godhead."[19] If the Kingship of the Son has no beginning and no end, at the conclusion of His redemptive work, Christ "will yield to the Father his name and crown of glory and whatever he has received from the Father...for to what purpose were power and lordship given to Christ unless that by his hand the Father might govern us?"[20] This is one of the more elliptic aspects of Calvin's teaching. In spite of his legendary caution, it serves to indicate that the movement begun in creation will one day reach its terminus.

This section has served to show that union with Christ is a central focus for Calvin. We have already seen to some measure that this union concerns the living, risen Christ, that it is intimate and physical as well as spiritual, that it implies action on the part of the Father and the Spirit, and that Christ is the source of new life through faith in the gospel, a faith that is diversely instrumental in the twofold grace.

---

18. Wendel, *Calvin*, 241f.

19. *Commentary* on 1 Corinthians 15:28.

20. *Inst.* 2.14.3. This finality has begun already under the reign of Christ, Calvin says in *Commentary* on 1 Corinthians 15:24.

Rather than continuing along this track, a rather well-worn path, I propose a different approach.[21]

Calvin's Use of Biblical Language

Union with Christ is presented in a rich and varied bouquet of language in the New Testament texts. "What Scripture tells us of this mystical union goes far beyond moral agreement in will and disposition," says Herman Bavinck. "It expressly states that Christ lives and dwells in believers and that they exist in him. The two are united as branch and vine, as are head and member, husband and wife, cornerstone and building."[22] This complex relationship is described in a variety of metaphors. Since it is virtually impossible to be exhaustive, I have chosen three metaphors that are evocative for Calvin: participation, adoption, and engrafting. Participation may well be considered as involving the two others and perhaps is fundamental.[23] It implies communion (*koinonia*) and fellowship in the body of Christ. Adoption is an act of God that issues in participation in Christ and His benefits, while engrafting describes the living union and the source of new life that partakes in Christ.

Insofar as texts are concerned, the choice is difficult because of the vast range of Calvin's biblical commentaries and sermons. However, two works stand out: the commentaries on Romans and John. Calvin no doubt worked concurrently on the second edition of his *Institutes* (1539) and the Romans commentary, his first (1540). The commentary on John came later (1553) and was dedicated to the syndics of the Geneva Council. In his preface, Calvin states that this commentary is the key to gaining understanding of the other Gospels, because John gives a living portrait of the power of Christ. Here, says Calvin, we

21. Cf. Christian Adjemian, "L'union en Christ chez Calvin," in *L'actualité de Jean Calvin* (Lausanne: L'Age d'Homme, 2008), 177–200.

22. Herman Bavinck, *Reformed Dogmatics* (Grand Rapids: Baker, 2008), 4:251.

23. Billings, *Calvin*, chap. 3.

find Christ as the pledge of God's paternal mercy toward us and His pledge to fulfil the office of the Mediator.[24]

Calvin comments on engrafting in John 15:1–11, on participation in Christ in Romans 6:1–11, and on adoption in Romans 8:13–17. In examining these passages, I will refer not to Calvin's exegetical method or to his explanation as a whole, but will limit myself to aspects concerning union with Christ.

Engrafting into Christ: John 15:1–11

We are engrafted into the true vine (v. 1). Calvin writes, "Ever since Christ has engrafted us into his body we, who are his members, must take special care not to disfigure ourselves with any spot or blemish."[25] Our vital sap, that is, all life and strength, comes from Christ alone.[26] Commenting on the opening verse of John 15, Calvin says, "We are by nature barren and dry, except in so far as we have been grafted into Christ and draw a power from him that is new." The nature of man is unfruitful and destitute of good "because no man has the nature of a vine until he is grafted in Christ, which is given to the elect alone by special grace." Commenting on verse 5, "without me ye can do nothing," Calvin removes the "sophistic objection" that if we can do nothing without Christ we may do something meritorious with Him by saying pertly that "without me" means "except from me." He goes on to say that by nature we are nothing and "begin to become vines when we are united to him to draw our strength from him."[27]

So Calvin underlines that spiritual life can come only from Christ in union with Him, and that life begins with engrafting. As a result, new life in Christ means that once we are engrafted into Him, we are dependent on Him for vitality. The principle is that our life is now in

24. *Commentary Evangile selon Jean* (Aix-en-Provence: Kerygma, 1978), 10–11. In the following quotations of John and Romans, I am translating freely from the French edition.

25. *Inst.* 3.6.3.

26. See also *Commentary* on Romans 5:6; 7:4; 13:14.

27. *Commentary* on John 15:1–5.

Him, because of Him. In other words, being united to Christ is life because of what He is in His life-giving power.

Calvin's interpretation of the "true vine" is striking. He opts for the translation "I am the vineyard," which means that those who are in Him are the vines planted there. In this perspective, Christ is the true vineyard in contrast with the degenerate Israel.[28] By implication, those who are planted in Him are the new Israel, although Calvin does not explicitly say so. In this passage, Christ is speaking primarily to His apostles, who will be hated by the world like their Master but who are His "friends" as they are called to make known all the things Christ has heard from the Father (v. 15). This means, according to Calvin, that since the wisdom of God is incomprehensible, He has limited His disclosure to things concerning the person and the office of the Mediator, "who places himself between God and us, having received out of the secret sanctuary of God those things which he should deliver to us."[29] Nothing important for salvation is omitted in the work of Christ. The uniqueness of Christ's mediatorial function in revelation dictates that His followers are to remain rooted in Him and in His truth and love to accomplish their task. We can extrapolate that the church is apostolic if it remains rooted in the truth, as the apostles are exhorted to do.

Christ presents Himself, then, according to Calvin, as the true field in which we are to remain rooted, like vines, in order to draw our life energy from Him. All other fields are barren. Calvin says this comparison means that we have no power of good apart from Christ, that being rooted in Christ we are cultivated and pruned by the Father, and that unfruitful vines are burned. Here is his conclusion:

> The first author of all good is the Father who has planted us by his hand; and the beginning of life is in Christ, when we begin to take root in him. When Christ calls himself the true vine it is as if he had said "I am truly the vine and men work in vain to find

28. Calvin refers to Isaiah 5:1ff; Jeremiah 2:21; Ezekiel 15:1ff.

29. *Commentary* on John 15:15.

life elsewhere. In fact no good fruit can be produced other than by vines that bear fruit in me."[30]

The mediatorial function of Christ is again in evidence, since the vines are in Christ because of the Father, the Husbandman who has planted them there. The fruit comes from life in Christ when the Father does the planting and the pruning. On Jesus' statement, "Every branch that beareth fruit, he purgeth it," Calvin comments:

> The faithful need assiduous cultivation if they are not to become wayward (*bâtards*) since they cannot produce any good unless God prunes them often. It is not enough that we have been once made participants in adoption if our good Lord does not continue working grace in us.[31]

How is the cleansing accomplished? "Now ye are clean" means, according to Calvin, that the disciples had already experienced pruning when they were planted in Christ. They were already cleansed or pruned by His Word, by His preaching. The truth (*doctrine*) of the gospel resembles the "vine dresser's knife to take away what is useless."[32] Calvin, being Calvin, cannot avoid saying here that the word proceeding from the mouth of man has no great efficacy, but "so far as Christ works in the heart by the Spirit, the word itself is the instrument of cleansing."[33]

Having root in the vine is all-important. To the question of whether any can be found in the vineyard that do not produce fruit, Calvin answers that this may be true of those who are reputed to be part of the church by external confession; hence the exhortation to "Abide in him." Continuance in grace through the Word is absolutely necessary. Christ promises that all who have a living root in Him will be fruit-bearing vines and that "the Spirit will always be efficacious in them."[34] The elect will never dry up because vitality flowing from

30. *Commentary* on John 15:1.

31. *Commentary* on John 15:2. This is the background for the teaching on suffering in the Christian life in *Inst.* 3.6–11.

32. *Commentary* on John 15:3.

33. Ibid.

34. *Commentary* on John 15:6.

Christ will continue. Even if there are "many hypocrites who in outward appearance flourish and are green for a while, afterwards, when they ought to yield fruit, they show a complete contrast to what the Lord expects and requires of his people."[35] So unfruitful branches, not pruned but judged by the Word, are removed from Christ in judgment.[36] Calvin makes no comment on "men gathering and casting them into the fire" (v. 6).

Christ abides in us through the vital sap of the Spirit, which enables His words to bear fruit in His vines. So the love of God flows into the vines as they abide in His love. The love of God referred to is not the imminent, mysterious love, but a pledge of God's love for us in Christ. Commenting on verse 9, Calvin says:

> Christ testifies that the Father loves him as he is the head of the Church. If, apart from the mediator, we enquire how God loves us, we are faced with a labyrinth and will find neither entrance nor exit. We ought therefore to fix our eyes on Christ in whom are found the clear testimony and pledge of the love of God. For the love of God was fully poured out on him, that from him it might flow to his members.... So we contemplate in him, as in a mirror, God's paternal love for us because he is not loved apart or for himself, but in that he unites us to the Father with him.

Paradoxically, the love of God for the Son is accomplished through the Son showing His love in laying down His life (v. 13). God could have saved us with a word or a simple act of will, Calvin says, but for our benefit, "by not sparing his well-beloved Son, he testifies in his person how much he cares for our salvation."[37] If our hearts are not softened by the inestimable sweetness of divine love, they must be harder than stone.

This is the context of "abide in my love" (v. 9), which is not, according to Calvin, a feeling of love for God or others, but the continual enjoyment of that love with which Christ has loved us. It implies taking care not to neglect our rooting. If we are weak, we must heed

35. Ibid.

36. See *Commentary* on Romans 11:16–24.

37. *Commentary* on John 15:13.

Christ's exhortation to persevere in the love He has shown, praying that He will confirm us in His love. Prayer expresses faith, the means of perseverance in keeping Christ's commands. It unites "the undeserved love of Christ toward us with a good conscience and newness of life." The effect of Christ's love is that believers "answer their calling because they are led by the Spirit of adoption of free grace."[38]

To encourage faith and perseverance with regard to the commandments, Calvin adds that our Lord holds Himself out as a pattern to imitate: "In me, Christ says, is brightly displayed the resemblance of those things that I ask of you; for you see how I persevere in my course. My Father, too, has loved me not for a short time but his love toward me is constant. The conformity of the head and the members ought to retain our attention."[39] Thus arises the peace and joy that is "possessed by all that have been justified by faith."[40] Calvin introduces justification at this point with regard to the commandments because obedience relates to "righteousness being freely imputed by forgiveness and therefore works that deserve to be rejected as imperfect and unholy are made acceptable to God."[41] Thus, the desire to live a holy life does not exclude what Calvin calls "the chief article of doctrine," the free pardon of justification, but is founded on it.

Calvin's exposition is a *tour de force*. It is simple and direct but profound, knitting together the main aspects and benefits of union with Christ. The whole structure is not grounded in a mystical identification, but is characterized by the centrality of the Mediator. The free pardon of grace and holiness is one with a faith that perseveres, being received through hearing the Word and made effective by the Spirit of adoption, who impresses on us the love of God in Christ. Fruitful vines in the vineyard are planted in Christ and receive sap from their rooting. Between the vines and the Husbandman is the third element, the vineyard. We could no more think of human beings

38. *Commentary* on John 15:9.
39. *Commentary* on John 15:10.
40. Ibid.
41. Ibid.

having a direct relation with God than we could imagine vines planted in mid-air.

Participation in Christ: Romans 6:1–11

Calvin places his cards on the table in the first lines of his commentary on Romans 6. Partaking in Christ, as in John 15, means the whole Christ, not a divided Christ, he says. It is impossible to imagine "free justice given to us apart from newness of life."[42] In systematic terms, justification and sanctification belong together and both are tributary of union with Christ.

Calvin uses "participation"[43] or its derivatives at least eight times in this section:

- Christ cleanses us by His blood and renders God propitious to us in expiation by making us partakers of His Spirit (v. 2).
- When we become partakers in the grace of Christ, the efficacy of His death appears immediately (v. 3).
- The death of Christ destroys the depravity of the flesh, while His resurrection effects the renovation of a better nature; by baptism we are admitted into participation in this grace (v. 4).
- Engrafting, a secret union, makes us partakers of the life no less than of the death of Christ (v. 5).
- We cannot be put to death other than by partaking in His death (v. 6).
- Christians must show evidence of participation in Christ's death (v. 7).

42. *Commentary* on Romans 6:1.

43. Calvin often uses "participation" in French in conjunction with words such as "communication" (communion), "société," or "union." The words "likeness" or "in common with Christ," which express the same idea, are also used. To simply take "participation" as fellowship, however, falls short of the intimacy of the union "participation" suggests. Such language also has a sacramental tone. Cf. Marijn De Kroon, *The Honour of God and Human Salvation: Calvin's Theology According to His Institutes* (Edinburgh: T & T Clark, 2001), 19–20, and Wendel, *Calvin,* 259.

- The bearing of the cross is followed by a participation in eternal life (v. 7).
- We cannot be participants in Christ except in newness of life, since He lives an incorruptible life (v. 8).

All these points refer in one way or another to the death and resurrection of Christ and our identity with Him in those acts. Insofar as He "was delivered up for our trespasses and raised for our justification" (Rom. 4:25), participation in Christ, which includes newness of life from sin and death, cannot exist without the double grace of justification and sanctification expressing that union. We are united with Christ in His death and resurrection.

As with the disposition of sanctification and justification in the structure of Book Three of the *Institutes*, where he deals with newness of life before he deals with justification, Calvin is concerned here with the "outrageous madness" of thinking that free grace in justification might foster sin. "By no means" (v. 2)! The opposite is true, Calvin claims: "If we have died to sin through the grace of Christ, then it is false to think that what abolishes sin could give vigour to it."[44] So the death of Christ, cleansing with His blood, and the propitiation of God, which together effect reconciliation, are never without the gift of regeneration that makes us partakers of the Spirit. Medicine that destroys disease does not nourish it. So we cannot still live in sin after we become dead to it, "sin" being taken by Calvin not in the sense of the guilt of sin but of its power. We are made partakers in the justice of Christ, adopted freely by grace, and therefore we can no longer walk in sin. The calling to holiness is rooted in justification and adoption.

Union with Christ is not possible without the destruction of sin. What is mainly to be considered in baptism is not simply washing and purification, Calvin says, but the "putting to death of the old man," and when we become one with Christ, "the efficacy of his death appears."[45] The effect of baptism is that "we become one with him:

44. *Commentary* on Romans 6:2.
45. *Commentary* on Romans 6:4.

being dead to ourselves, we become new creatures."[46] The truth of baptism is ratified by faith, through which believers put on Christ (cf. Gal. 3:27). Thus, the power of God is revealed in all the fruits of the resurrection of Christ. So a transition is made from participation in death to participation in life: "The old man is destroyed by the death of Christ and his resurrection brings justice and makes us new creatures."[47] This is an indissoluble link: "The death of Christ is efficacious to destroy and demolish the depravity of our flesh and the resurrection to effect the state of a new and better nature."[48]

In the subsequent verses, the language of "grafting" or "planting" is used.[49] As in his interpretation of John 15, Calvin states that this language is not exemplary but describes "the secret union of his Spirit, by which his power flows in us so we partake in the life of Christ." The death of our present life is similar to the death of Christ in that it means spiritual renewal. "Grafted" indicates not something required of us but the benefit we derive from Christ because of "the grafting made by the hand of God." Not only are we nourished by Christ, we "pass from our nature to his nature" and the "efficacy of his resurrection renews in us a spiritual nature." Thus, we are delivered as crucified from the bondage of sin.

Verses 7 to 11 are an application of the consequences of dying with Christ. Death destroys all the actions of this life, freeing and absolving us (*justifie du péché*) from them. Participation in the death of Christ brings an end to sin, and the work of God already begun advances daily and is by degrees brought to its finality in our participation with Christ in eternal life. Dying is done with once and for all, but living with Christ is continuous through participation in His incorruptible life. Calvin's summary is: "Christ now makes the faithful alive and by his Spirit breathes his own life into them by his secret power from heaven; as he was liberated from the power of death so he liberates

46. Ibid.
47. Ibid.
48. Ibid.
49. *Commentary* on Romans 6:5–8.

all those who belong to him."[50] So there is a likeness between what happened to Christ and what happens to us. Calvin's commentary on Romans 6:10 shows that Christ made Himself a ransom for sin and died once to obtain eternal redemption through expiation for sin by His blood. Just as He reconciles us by His blood to the Father, He regenerates us at the same time by the power of His Spirit.[51]

The conclusion of Calvin's comments is pastoral, as befits the tone of verse 11:

> Think of how it is in you: as once Christ died to destroy sin, so you died once that in future you cease from sinning. You must continue the mortification that has been begun until sin is once and for all abolished. As Christ was raised to an incorruptible life, so by the grace of God you are also born anew, that you may live all your life in holiness and righteousness inasmuch as the power of the Holy Spirit, by which you are renewed is eternal and shall ever continue the same.[52]

Calvin is not a modern exegete, and his interpretation of union with Christ as participation in Christ does not have the sharpness of redemptive-historical *einmalig* interpretation, although Herman Ridderbos followed Calvin in using the language of participation: "Baptism incorporates us into, makes us participate in, Christ's death on Golgotha and resurrection in the garden."[53] Calvin's concern is biblical, but as a humanist, he also has an eye on the patristic tradition.[54] For Calvin, participation in Christ means union in terms of possession of the benefits wrought by Christ in His work of redemption. This

---

50. *Commentary* on Romans 6:9.

51. Calvin comments on this passage in *Inst.* 4.15.5–6 when he speaks of the three consolations of baptism, the third being the attestation of our union with Christ.

52. *Commentary* on Romans 6:11.

53. Herman Ridderbos, *Paul: An Outline of His Theology* (Grand Rapids: Eerdmans, 1973), 403–5.

54. As Billings ably shows, *Calvin*, 14ff. Cf. particularly Dennis E. Tamburello, *Union with Christ: John Calvin and the Mysticism of St. Bernard* (Louisville, Ky.: Westminster/John Knox, 1994), chap. 1; A. N. S. Lane, *John Calvin: Student of the Church Fathers* (Edinburgh: T & T Clark, 1999), chaps. 1, 2, 5.

view is closer to Ridderbos' construal than to mystical approaches or ideas of deification. Rather than rest and repose, it has a tone of struggle and conflict that characterizes chapters 6–11 of the *Institutes,* Book Three.

As we have seen, participation in Christ implies the realization of the twofold grace in the believer's life. One cannot be in Christ unless one partakes of the righteousness and holiness implied in His death for sin and His living to righteousness. So what happened in Christ becomes true in and of the believer, because through participation it is mirrored in his experience. The expressions, we "pass from our nature to his nature" and the "efficacy of his resurrection renews in us a spiritual nature," describe participation very well. Here we have, it seems, a "triangulation" involving union, justification, and sanctification.[55] As Calvin says:

> Why then are we justified by faith? Because by faith we grasp Christ's righteousness, by which alone we are reconciled to God. Yet you could not grasp this without at the same time grasping sanctification also.... Therefore Christ justifies no one whom he does not at the same time sanctify. These benefits are joined together by an everlasting and indissoluble bond, so that those whom he illumines by his wisdom he redeems; those whom he redeems he justifies, those whom he justifies he sanctifies.... Do you wish to attain righteousness in Christ? You must first possess Christ; but you cannot possess him without being made partaker in his sanctification, because he cannot be divided into pieces.[56]

Adoption: Romans 8:13–17

Union with Christ is the closest of relations, involving engrafting into His body and participation in a common life in which Christ dwells in us:

> Let us know the unity we have with our Lord Jesus Christ: he wills to have a common life with us, and that what he has should be ours: nay, that he even wishes to dwell in us, not in

55. Gaffin, "Justification," 268–69.

56. *Inst.* 3.16.1.

> imagination but in effect; not in earthly fashion but spiritually; and that whatever may befall, he so labours by virtue of his Holy Spirit that we are united with him more closely than are limbs with the body.[57]

The intimacy of union with Christ also involves partaking in Christ's Sonship. There is, therefore, a link between union with Christ and adoption. In fact, just as union with Christ is inconceivable without engrafting into and participation in Christ's life, it is equally inconceivable without adoption. We are not naturally members of God's family but children of wrath. In Christ, the Son, we are adopted into the family to become sons of God. Adoption is close to justification and similarly shows that union with Christ is forensic as well as vital. As in justification we are exonerated by God the Judge because of Christ, so in adoption we are made sons of the Father because of the Son.

Romans 8 might be seen as a series of litmus tests revealing the presence of new life in Christ that characterizes believers. A consciousness of sonship is one such evidence, and it is developed in these verses. As we already have seen, just as participation in Christ is conjoined in justification and sanctification, so also there is no sonship without the twofold grace. Calvin states:

> There is no trust in God, where there is no love of justice. I take as evident that we are justified in Christ through the grace (*miséricorde*) of God alone; but equally certain is the fact that all who are justified are called to live according to the holy calling of God. Let the faithful learn to embrace Christ not only in justification (*justice*) but also in sanctification so as not to divide him by half-faith.[58]

How is this trust obtained? It comes through the leading of the Spirit, who makes us sons: "Those alone who are led by the spirit are children of God, because this is the mark by which God recognises his own...children of God who are led by his Spirit are heirs to eternal life...and ought to feel assured of eternal life." Calvin calls this a

57. "9th Sermon on the Passion," *Opp.*, 46, 953, quoted by Wendel, *Calvin*, 235.

58. *Commentary* on Romans 8:13.

special dispensation of the Spirit and states that by sanctification "the Lord favours none but his own elect, and by this he separates them from others to be numbered with his sons."[59]

In Calvin's commentary on Romans 8:13–17, we find an implicit order of salvation underlying the exhortation to live in holiness of life. Election implies sonship and separation, and justification and sanctification are united in the calling to live in Christ. Union with Christ is variously expressed in the different aspects of the *ordo salutis.*

The assurance of faith has to do with the special work of the Spirit, which impresses on us the paternal mercy of God in forgiving our infirmities and indwelling sins: "Our confidence in this respect is made certain by the Spirit of adoption who could not inspire us with trust in prayer without sealing in us the gratuitous forgiveness God has granted us." Contrary to a spirit of bondage proceeding from the law, this is the spirit of adoption from the gospel and the priceless benefit the Son of God has brought us through it. How is this benefit applied? "Christ, the heavenly teacher, not only addresses the faithful by words, but also teaches them inwardly and effectually by his Spirit."

If, under the law, the godly "were illuminated by the same Spirit of faith and had the hope of eternal life which the Spirit as the earnest sealed in their hearts," under the gospel "the Spirit is more largely and abundantly poured forth under the reign of Christ."[60] So now through the gospel "the Spirit of adoption exhilarates our souls by witnessing to our salvation."[61] Through this Spirit we call God Father. Once again, if the faithful under the law called God Father, Calvin says, it was not with such great confidence because the veil kept them at a distance from the Holy of Holies. But now, "since an entrance has been opened to us by the blood of Christ, we may rejoice fully and freely that we are children of God." This is because "God forgives us our sin and deals kindly with us as the Father of his children."[62]

59. *Commentary* on Romans 8:14.

60. Ibid.

61. Ibid.

62. Ibid.

Adoption to sonship is the special work of "the Spirit himself," as verse 14 states. Calvin calls the Spirit our "guide and teacher," paralleling the work of Christ, "the heavenly" teacher. Our spirits are incapable of assurance with regard to sonship, but the Spirit "pours into our hearts such confidence that we venture to call God our Father" and "testifies to our heart respecting the paternal love of God."[63] Without this assurance, Calvin says, there is no true calling on God in prayer. True faith is evidenced by supplication, and exercise in prayer shows the reality of faith because of trust in God's promises.

In verse 17, adoption to divine sonship, the special work of the Spirit, appears to be grounded in Christ. Salvation consists in having God as Father and being adopted as His children, but this implies an inheritance that is held in common with the Son:

> God has adopted us as his children and has at the same time ordained an inheritance for us...a heavenly, incorruptible and eternal inheritance, such as is possessed by Christ...and the excellence of this inheritance is shown in that we partake of it in common with the only begotten Son of God.[64]

The present, vital, and practical aspects of union with Christ are finely stated when Calvin comments on "coheritors with Christ if we suffer with him to be glorified with him" (v. 17):

> We are coheritors with Christ, provided that we follow him on the same path he took in order to enter into the inheritance.... God's inheritance is ours because by his grace he has adopted us to be his children. And so that we may not doubt its possession has been already conferred on Christ with whom we have been made co-owners and partners. Christ came into it by the cross and we must enter into it by the same way.[65]

This does not open the door to salvation by works. In the *Institutes*, Calvin says that we should not "exempt ourselves from the condition to which Christ our Head had to submit, especially since he submitted to it for our sake, to show an example of patience in

---

63. Ibid.

64. *Commentary* on Romans 8:17.

65. Ibid. Cf. *Inst.* 3.8.

himself."[66] Likewise, Calvin speaks in his commentary of the order by which God dispenses salvation to us and not its cause. Salvation in Christ is by free grace, not works; here the way of the cross shows how God governs His people. Further on, in his comments on verses 26–27, Calvin speaks of the way of the Spirit with us: If we should find our crosses too heavy to bear, the "Spirit himself takes on the weight of our burden by which we, in our weakness, are oppressed, and not only does he help and succour us but he also lifts us up, as if he carried our burden with us."[67]

In conclusion, the Holy Spirit is the bond that unites believers to the Son. Adoption makes believers sons of the Father in the Son. By this act, they become co-inheritors with the Son. However, there is an observable order. It is because of the redemption accomplished by the Son that believers receive the Spirit of adoption. The living experience of assurance in faith, trust, and prayer, obtained by the witness of the Spirit, makes us one with Christ in His inheritance. This inheritance is obtained by His blood, which pays the price for the ransom of sins. The sanctifying and succouring work of the Spirit unites us to Christ, in whom justification and sanctification have their ground.

Conclusion

In Calvin's thought, union with Christ is the heart of the gospel. The incarnation of Christ is the focus of the triune God in His acts of salvation, and union with Christ is the operational focus. The Father is the author of life and of election, the One who justifies and adopts on the basis of the imputation of Christ's righteousness.

In Christ we find the fountain of life, for He is the Mediator to whom we are united in His death and resurrection, issuing in newness of life. The Spirit seals the Word of truth in our hearts, bears witness to Christ, and is the abiding principle of communion with Christ. From day to day, the Spirit accompanies and mediates the grace of God in Christ to us.

66. *Inst.* 3.8.1.

67. *Commentary* on Romans 8:26.

Union with Christ is also central, as we have seen, because it is articulated in harmony with the double grace flowing from the work of Christ—justification and sanctification. The two graces make the potential benefits of Christ actual in the lives of believers. We possess nothing until we are "engrafted into" Christ, until we "put on Christ" and are made "one body" with Him, becoming sons of the Father through the secret work of the Spirit. So "we come to enjoy Christ and all his benefits."[68] None of the benefits of the *ordo salutis* are possible outside of union with Christ.

Union with Christ is spiritual and mystical because of Calvin's articulation of it in terms of participation, engrafting, and adoption. However, it remains foreign to the mysticism or deification found in other traditions, because Christ alone is the Mediator between God and man, and it is only in terms of His mediation that the union is construed. In summarizing Calvin, Joel Beeke writes: "Such a union is possible because Christ took on our human nature, filling it with his virtue. Union with Christ in his humanity is historical, ethical, and personal, but not essential.... We are not absorbed into Christ, not united to him in such a way that our human personalities are annulled even in the slightest degree."[69]

Finally, we are united to Christ not just as spirit to Spirit but also, mysteriously, in a bodily sense. As the fountain of life, the risen Christ is the source of present bodily life in the flesh. For Calvin, as our bodies are animated by our souls, so the living Christ becomes the principle of our life, for our bodies are "members of Christ":

> The spiritual union we have with Christ belongs not only to the soul, but also to the body, so much so that we are flesh of his flesh and bone of his bone (Eph. 5:30). Otherwise the hope of the resurrection would be faint indeed were not our union what it is: namely complete and entire.[70]

---

68. *Inst.* 3.1.1.

69. Joel R. Beeke, "Appropriating Salvation," in *A Theological Guide to Calvin's Institutes*, 272.

70. *Commentary* on 1 Corinthians 6:19. Cf. *Inst.* 4.17.8–9.

Union with Christ, then, is a Spirit-forged reality by which we on earth are united to the living, risen, eternal Christ in heaven. This became the governing perspective of Calvin's sacramental theology, developed in the *Institutes,* Book Four:

> This is the wonderful exchange which, out of his measureless benevolence he has made with us; that, becoming Son of man with us, he has made us sons of God with him; that, by his descent to earth, he has prepared an ascent to heaven for us;...that, accepting our weakness, he has strengthened us by his power; that, receiving our poverty unto himself, he has transferred his wealth to us; that, taking the weight of our iniquity upon himself (which oppressed us), he has clothed us with his righteousness.[71]

71. *Inst.* 4.17.2.

CHAPTER 5

Calvin and Christian Experience: The Holy Spirit in the Life of the Christian

Sinclair B. Ferguson

The century since the four hundredth anniversary of the birth of John Calvin has witnessed many developments in the story of the Christian church, but few have been more striking than the avalanche of new interest in the ministry of the Holy Spirit. It might be thought that this interest provides the major stimulus for a chapter that might exhaust the (presumably) little that Calvin had to say on the subject. But it would be a mistake, on more than one count, to imagine that Calvin's references to the Spirit were sparse. Indeed, already in 1909, B. B. Warfield was prepared to venture the thesis that Calvin was "preeminently the theologian of the Holy Spirit."[1]

Warfield may have been one of only a few voices crying in the wilderness, but his assessment is vindicated in a number of ways, for Calvin's writings abound in references to the person and ministry of the Spirit. For such a profoundly biblical theologian, it could not be otherwise. As Calvin worked his way through biblical revelation, he emphasized the multidimensional character of the Spirit's role. His understanding of the Spirit's work ranged from His involvement in the creating and governing of the universe, to the giving and authenticating of Scripture to believers, to His presence in the ministry of our Lord Jesus Christ. Then, since the Holy Spirit is the bond of union between Jesus Christ and the whole church as well as the individual believer, Calvin further traced His activity in the application of the redemption

1. B. B. Warfield, *Calvin as a Theologian and Calvin Today* (Philadelphia: Presbyterian Board of Publication, 1909). Warfield's view was probably shared by few theologians of his day.

that Christ accomplished.[2] Thus, throughout his biblical commentaries and *The Institutes of the Christian Religion*, he underscored that the Holy Spirit is the key to the church's communion with the Lord Jesus, not least (as we shall see) in the Lord's Supper.

This is not to claim that the work of the Holy Spirit is the central motif in Calvin's theology; "all-pervasive" would be a better description of the reality.

It might be objected that while the *Institutes* contains sections on the work of God the Father (Book I) and the person and work of Jesus Christ (Book II), there is no distinct treatment of the Holy Spirit and His work. To some extent, this is explained by the fact that Calvin understood that the Holy Spirit does not bring glory to Himself but to the Father and to the Son.[3] Thus, references to the Holy Spirit and His work are pervasive throughout the entire encyclopedia of Calvin's thought rather than localized in one particular area of it. Indeed, such was the extent of his interest in this theme that it might be claimed that Calvin paved the way for the attention to the Spirit's ministry that would later mark evangelical theology. He, probably more than any other Reformer, bequeathed to the Reformed tradition the deep interest in the role of the Spirit that would come to prominence in such *magna opera* as John Owen and Thomas Goodwin's monumental studies in the Puritan era.[4]

In this context, it is necessary to limit comments to only a few aspects of Calvin's teaching.

---

2. See *Institutes of the Christian Religion*, Library of Christian Classics, vols. XX–XXI, ed. John T. McNeill, trans. Ford Lewis Battles (Louisville: Westminster John Knox, 1960), Book 3, Chapter 1, Section 3. Hereafter the format *Inst.* 3.1.3 will be used. Cf. John Calvin, *The Gospel according to St. John, 11–21*, ed. D. W. and T. F. Torrance, trans. T. H. L. Parker (Grand Rapids: Eerdmans, 1961), 121, on John 16:14.

3. "The Spirit bestows on us nothing apart from Christ." Calvin, *The Gospel according to St. John, 11–21*, 122.

4. John Owen, "*Pneumatologia*," in *The Works of John Owen*, ed. W. H. Goold, vols. 3–4 (Edinburgh: Johnstone and Hunter, 1850–52); Thomas Goodwin, "The Work of the Holy Ghost in our Salvation," in *The Works of Thomas Goodwin*, vol. 6 (London: James Nichol, 1863).

The Polemical Context

To understand what Calvin says about the ministry of the Spirit, we should first consider the polemical context in which he was writing.

On the one hand, he faced the necessity of dealing with Roman Catholic theology. In the late medieval church, salvation for a regular church member—if attainable at all—was dependent on the institutions of the church. In the view of the Reformers, for all practical purposes, the *magisterium* had replaced the Holy Spirit in His work of authenticating the Scriptures to the believer (the *testimonium internum Spiritus sancti* so beloved of Calvin[5]). Rome claimed that the church had created the canon of Scripture; therefore, the church authenticated Scripture and was its sole interpreter. By contrast, Calvin argued that the Scriptures were given by the Spirit and therefore were canonical from their moment of origin.[6] Furthermore, the Spirit continued to authenticate them to believers.[7] No merely human testimony can ever be adequate to bear witness to the divine nature of God's Word. Only God can give testimony to Himself, Calvin says, echoing Hilary of Poitiers.[8]

The tragedy of the medieval church, from Calvin's point of view, was not only the distortion of the gospel of free justification, but the usurpation of the ministry of the Holy Spirit in the application of redemption, replacing His dynamic activity with a static and formal sacramental *ordo salutis*. In that system, the ordinary Christian might hope to progress in grace, from being baptized into the church, through participating in the various church sacraments that would sustain him in life, so that one day he would become the kind of righteous person—his faith fully formed in unadulterated love for God (*fides formata caritate*)—whom God could then justify because he was in fact righteous.[9]

5. See *Inst.* 1.7.4.
6. *Inst.* 1.7.1.
7. *Inst.* 1.7.4.
8. Ibid.
9. *Inst.* 3.15.7.

From within this system of justification, the Roman Catholic Church accused the Reformers of teaching a legal fiction (the justification of the *unjust*). Calvin both demonstrated the biblical basis for such justification and the fact that rather than making room for license as a legal fiction, its actual effect through the Spirit was to spur the justified on to greater godliness.[10]

Since, for Calvin, the justification of the ungodly is based solely on the justification accomplished in Jesus Christ acting for us, the great work of the Holy Spirit is to unite us to Christ, in whom this justification is grounded, and in union with whom sanctification is effected and develops. Moral license is impossible, for the Spirit unites us to Christ as Savior and Lord—to have Him as one but not the other is, as Calvin puts it, "to rend Christ asunder."[11]

Thus, we might add to the customary *solas* of the Reformation the principle that the salvation that is in Christ alone, by grace alone, by faith alone, is also "by the Spirit alone."

If this first aspect of Calvin's polemic dealt with the way the Roman church replaced the Spirit's ministry with the sacramental system, the second aspect involved the radical groups of the so-called "left wing" of the Reformation, whom Calvin saw falling into the error of dividing the Spirit from the Word. These groups separated the Spirit from the Word by emphasizing that God reveals Himself through the Spirit *apart from* the Word. Calvin speaks of their "fatal fantasies in which fanatics entangle themselves when they abandon the Word and invent some sort of vague and erratic spirit."[12]

The refrain that runs through Calvin's teaching in this context is that the Spirit is never to be separated from Christ, nor should He be separated from the Word. In 1545, Calvin wrote a sharply worded tract, *Against the Fantastic and Furious Sect of the Libertines called Spirituals.* The telltale sign of their imbalance was that they could speak scarcely

10. John Calvin, *The Epistles of Paul the Apostle to the Romans and to the Thessalonians*, ed. D. W. and T. F. Torrance, trans. Ross Mackenzie (Grand Rapids: Eerdmans, 1961), 121.

11. Ibid. See also *Commentary on Romans,* 166–67.

12. John Calvin, *The Acts of the Apostles, 1–13*, eds. D. W. and T. F. Torrance, trans. J. W. Fraser and W. G. McDonald (Grand Rapids: Eerdmans, 1965), 317.

a few sentences without referring to the Holy Spirit and the leading or revelation He gave. Calvin viewed such language as a distortion of biblical teaching that resulted in harmful confusion about the Spirit's ministry: "For as soon as the Spirit is severed from Christ's Word the door is open to all sorts of craziness and impostures. Many fanatics have tried a similar method of deception in our own age. The written teaching seems to them to be of the letter. Therefore they were pleased to make up a new theology consisting of revelations."[13]

This supposed mark of higher spiritual maturity is actually a sign of spiritual neuroticism, because it severs the Spirit from the Word. What Calvin emphasized in contrast is the close union of the Father with the Son, the Son with the Spirit, and the Spirit with the Word, so that the ministry of all three persons of the Godhead is expressed through the Word as the Spirit brings believers into genuine union and communion with the Father and the Son.

The Theological Context

In the *Institutes*, Calvin emphasizes the deity of the Spirit in a manner consonant with the teaching of the fathers and creeds of antiquity. While in earlier life he seems to have wanted to keep within the confines of purely biblical language when expressing the mysteries of the gospel, he came to realize that the technical vocabulary of the early church provided a means by which doctrinal parameters could be set and an appropriate theological shorthand employed.[14]

The Spirit is a person of divine essence. He is a distinct center of personal existence within the single essence of the being of God. He reveals His divinity by participating in creation and providence, in sending prophets, and in the inspiration of Scripture. The Spirit possesses infinite knowledge of God. God is known exhaustively only to Himself, and the deep things of God are known by the Holy Spirit. When the New Testament speaks of believers corporately or

13. Calvin, *The Gospel according to St. John, 11–21*, 121.

14. See his discussion in *Inst.* 1.12.3. Cf. John Calvin, *The First Epistle of Paul the Apostle to the Corinthians*, ed. D. W. and T. F. Torrance, trans. J. W. Fraser (Grand Rapids: Eerdmans, 1960), 79.

individually as temples of God, it is because they are indwelt by the Holy Spirit. The inherent logic in those statements implies the absolute deity of the person of the Holy Spirit.[15]

The baptismal formula, Calvin argues, expresses not only the unity-in-trinity of God's being but the specific deity of the Spirit. The unity of God's name implies the unity of the persons in the triune God.[16]

Perhaps Calvin's most significant contribution to the development of the doctrine of the Trinity lay in his insistence on the auto-theistic nature of the Son—while the Father is the personal fountain of the Trinity in terms of the diversity of persons, the Son possesses His deity (as does the Father) in an underived fashion. The Father is not the author of the deity of the Son. It follows, then, that the Holy Spirit is also auto-theistic; His deity is not derived from the Father and from the Son. He is Himself very God of very God.[17] The Spirit is common to both the Father and the Son. He is one essence with Them, and is the same eternal deity while proceeding personally from both. Citing Romans 8:9, Calvin says the Spirit is as truly the Spirit of the Son as He is truly the Spirit of the Father. He proceeds personally from both the Father and the Son within the internal union and communion of the Trinity.[18] This reality is expressed by revelation when at Pentecost the Spirit is sent from both the Father and the Son to believers in the church.

The maxim *opera ad extra trinitatis indivisa sunt*[19] applies to His ministry in the believer. When the believer receives the Spirit, he also receives the Father and the Son. The Trinity is indivisible in all of

---

15. *Inst.* 1.13.14–15.

16. John Calvin, *Harmony of the Gospels Matthew, Mark and Luke*, ed. D. W. and T. F. Torrance, trans. A. W. Morrison (Grand Rapids: Eerdmans, 1972), 3.253.

17. See *Inst.* 1.13.16–20.

18. Calvin thus subscribes to the *filioque* clause in the Western form of the Nicene Creed. See *Inst.* 1.13.18.

19. The *ad extra* works of God are those He does in relation to His creation, not those which are within the trinty of Persons in the Godhead. The meaning of *opera ad extra trinitatis indivisa sunt* is that all God's *ad extra* works are joint undertakings of the three Persons.

God's activities beyond Himself, although for Calvin each person of the Trinity has specific roles in God's external relationship to the universe (the so-called doctrine of "appropriations").

Calvin traces the role of the Spirit not only in creation but through the old covenant into the new. In *Institutes* 2.11, he shows the contrast between the Spirit's roles in the Old Testament and New Testament epochs. But he also emphasizes that the Spirit who ministered to the saints under the old covenant and brought them to hope for redemption in Jesus Christ is the same Spirit who ministers to the saints under the new covenant and brings the consummation of that redemption to believers. Whether under the law or through its fulfillment in Jesus Christ, the Holy Spirit applies the work of Jesus Christ. The words of the prologue to John's Gospel, that the law came through Moses while grace and truth came through Jesus Christ (1:17), do not point so much to a radical antithesis between two dispensations with different agents in the application of redemption but to two dispensations of the same redemptive historical stream, the one finding its fulfillment and consummation in the other.[20]

The Holy Spirit applies the work of Jesus Christ to those who believe in Him, whether they see Him opaquely in terms of promise or live (as we do) in light of the historical reality of the death of Jesus. The Holy Spirit bridges the gap in space and time between the historical anticipation and the actual accomplishment of our Lord Jesus Christ's saving ministry and the present time, in which God justifies sinners and transforms them into saints. So while the Holy Spirit worked through the old covenant, His ministry came to marvelous consummation in the new covenant.

Against this general background, there are four areas in which Calvin particularly emphasizes the Spirit's ministry in the life of the Christian believer: illumination, regeneration, adoption, and communion. The dividing lines between these themes are thin, for they are tributaries feeding into one marvelous unity in Calvin's thinking.

20. See his discussion in *The Gospel according to St. John, 1–10*, ed. D. W. and T. F. Torrance, trans. T. H. L. Parker (Grand Rapids: Eerdmans, 1959), 24–25.

Illumination

The Spirit who gives us Scripture also convinces us of the truth of Scripture through that truth. We do not stand outside of Scripture to be convinced of its authority as the Word of God. Thus, for Calvin, we are ultimately persuaded that Scripture is God's Word not by the use of arguments extraneous to Scripture, nor by any of its impressive external characteristics, but by the reading and exposition of Scripture itself. The Holy Spirit uses the very Scriptures that we read to persuade us that what we are reading is the very Word of God. His testimony is not superimposed on the Word, but comes with and through the Word.[21] There is no substitute for this.

The implication of what Calvin is saying is that while Christians can commend the Bible in all kinds of ways, the fundamental need is for people to hear it or read it for themselves. "*Tolle lege*" ("Take up and read") is the watchword that will lead to the conversion of many, in addition to Augustine!

Calvin insists, then, that Scripture itself, through the ministry of the Spirit, brings inner certainty that it is the very voice of God, "as if there the living words of God were heard."[22] That is why the fruit of the Spirit's ministry is that we give to Scripture the reverence that we give to God Himself, because it is His own Word.

For Calvin, illumination involves more than understanding what Scripture says; it is an internal persuasion of, and a yielding to, its truth.

This perspective was rooted in Calvin's experience. At one time, of course, he was a convinced Roman Catholic ("stubbornly addicted" to the Roman Catholic Church, is his own way of describing his earlier life[23]). However, as the Scriptures were illumined to him by the Holy

21. *Inst.* 1.7.4.

22. *Inst.* 1.7.1.

23. See Calvin's comments in his introduction to his *Commentary on the Book of Psalms*, where he describes himself in this way: "Since I was too obstinately devoted to the superstitions of Popery to be easily extricated from so profound an abyss of mire, God by a sudden conversion subdued and brought my mind to a teachable frame, which was more hardened in such matters than might have been expected from one at my early period of life." John Calvin, *Commentary on the*

Spirit, Calvin began yielding to a greater authority than the church or his own prejudice. But he also learned that inner illumination is not a substitute for external and objective revelation. Indeed, it is impossible apart from it, for the Spirit must never be separated from the Word, since the Spirit gives the Word so that He might illumine the Word, breaking down the stubborn prejudices of our nature, which, as Calvin says, is "a perpetual factory of idols."[24] The Spirit engages in a demolition and reconstruction process in the mind as light enters into it from the teaching of Scripture. This is what happened to the disciples on the road to Emmaus (Luke 24:13–35). Jesus opened the Scriptures to them. There was both light (illumination) and heat (burning hearts).[25]

The Spirit's work in illumination is an integral aspect of regeneration. Those who are born again "see" the kingdom of God (John 3:3). The Spirit enlightens the mind, reveals Christ, subdues the heart, and makes the heart burn. Being convinced of the Scriptures this way is not merely a scholastic conviction. Rather, the testimony of the Holy Spirit is so intertwined with the grasp of the truth of the gospel that it is indistinguishable from it in actual regeneration.

The Spirit of illumination is therefore also the Spirit of regeneration. But this, for Calvin, is a broad category and requires separate consideration.

Regeneration

Here contemporary readers of Calvin may misread him. The progression of Calvin's exposition of "The Way in Which We Receive the Grace of Christ" in *Institutes* Book 3 contrasts with the order of exposition characteristic of later Reformed theology. There, regeneration is viewed as the prerequisite for faith, justification, adoption, sanctification, and perseverance, and therefore is given priority over them in the order of exposition (as well as in the *ordo salutis*).

Book of Psalms, trans. James Anderson (Edinburgh: Calvin Translation Society, 1843–55), 1:xl.

24. *Inst.* 1.11.8.

25. Calvin, *Harmony of the Gospels Matthew, Mark and Luke*, 3.238.

Against this background, the reader who comes to Calvin as the fountain of the Reformed understanding of the *ordo salutis* is likely to experience something of a shock. He essentially deals with sanctification *before* he deals with justification, and in that context he uses the expression "regeneration by faith," which has, to modern ears, a distinctly Arminian ring!

What is Calvin about in Book 3 of the *Institutes* that might help to explain this? Two things in particular are of interest at this point:

First, part of Calvin's motivation in discussing the Christian life *prior* to discussing justification is to provide theological grounding for his conviction that there is no such thing as a justified man who is not also a sanctified man. Justification is never grounded in sanctification. Justification must never be confused with sanctification. But neither can justification ever exist without sanctification. In the Roman polemic (to which Calvin was extremely sensitive from the very beginning of his ministry), free justification of the ungodly by grace alone through faith alone inevitably leads to libertinism. Since the same accusation was leveled against Paul (Rom. 6:1ff), its reappearance in the sixteenth century simply confirmed to Calvin that his gospel was faithful to the apostolic teaching.[26] It need hardly be said that Calvin did not advocate, nor did his gospel encourage, antinomianism any more than did the apostle Paul.

Second, and more fundamentally, Calvin uses the term *regeneration* in a different way from the customary usage of later Reformed theology. For him, the regeneration that comes through faith is repentance.[27] Repentance, in turn, is that lifelong mortification and vivification, both internal and external, that characterizes the whole of the Christian life.

In a word, Calvin has a much more unified idea of what happens in regeneration than later theologians, who tend to speak about regeneration as the inauguration point in the Christian life, an initial and instantaneous work of God rather than an ongoing transformation. But for Calvin, regeneration or repentance is much more than the

26. See Calvin, *Commentary on Romans*, 63–64.

27. *Inst.* 3.3.

event of a moment; it is the ongoing restoration of a person's whole being into the image of God. In this, Calvin echoes the first of Martin Luther's Ninety-five Theses: "When our Lord Jesus Christ said 'repent' he meant that the whole of the Christian life should be repentance."

This helps us make sense of a number of things Calvin writes. For example, in his discussion of John 1:12 ("as many as received him, to them gave he power to become the sons of God..."), he speaks of regeneration preceding faith and also of regeneration following faith.[28] Does Calvin speak with a forked tongue? No, he means that the regenerating activity of God the Holy Spirit is absolutely essential to the birth of faith in our lives, the sovereign ministry of illumination through the Word of God, conviction of its truth, and the enflaming of the heart. We must be born from above. But divine regeneration, which is sovereignly inaugurated, is also continued in the Christian life by the way of faith, because what God has in view is the regeneration of our entire lives—which ultimately will be climaxed in that *vivificatio externa* (external vivification) that will take place in the final resurrection of the body. Thus, regeneration is consummated in final Christ-likeness and glorification. It is an ongoing process in the Christian life. It takes place *in* my life in a way that engages my being, so that I actually *am made new and become new* in every aspect of life. In this sense, there is both divine monergism and also a kind of synergism in the actual experience of salvation. The person who is made new actually does new things—they do not simply "happen" above his head.[29]

Calvin's commentary on John 1:13 makes it clear that this is how he understands regeneration. The Holy Spirit, in essence, unites us by faith with the Lord Jesus Christ so that we become one with Him and His life comes to expression in ours.

We share in Christ by participation. This language is significant for Calvin, because salvation comes to us not only *from* Christ as its

28. Calvin, *The Gospel according to St. John, 1–10*, 18–19.

29. Cf. John Calvin, *The Epistles of Paul the Apostle to the Galatians, Philippians, Ephesians and Colossians*, ed. D. W. and T. F. Torrance, trans. T. H. L. Parker (Grand Rapids: Eerdmans, 1965), 253–56.

source, or *through* Christ as the channel, but *in* Christ. Indeed, the prepositional distinction is so significant for Calvin that on more than one occasion he writes in such terms as: "I prefer however to retain Paul's words *in* Christ Jesus rather than to render with Erasmus *by* Christ Jesus, because this conveys more clearly the ingrafting by which we are made one with Christ."[30] For Calvin, we do not gain the blessings of the Christian gospel merely *through* Christ, as though they were entities somehow capable of impersonal abstraction from Him. Rather, all of the blessings come in Him.

In essence, Calvin is emphasizing here that it is Jesus Christ—not justification, regeneration, sanctification, glorification, or adoption as such—that we need. None of these is the object of Spirit-wrought faith. Rather, through the Holy Spirit, faith unites us to Jesus Christ in a spiritual but real union, and we receive all these blessings in Him, not apart from Him. This is everything to Calvin.[31]

But the fact that this is the work of the Spirit does not mean that spiritual blessings come from a *mystical* Christ. Rather, they are embodied for us in the incarnate, crucified, buried, raised, ascended, and glorified Christ who forever retains our humanity. He is the One to whom we are united. We are not united *to* the Holy Spirit. We are united *by* the Holy Spirit to the person of our Lord Jesus Christ.

This is the key to what Calvin writes about the Spirit's ministry, especially in *Institutes,* Book 3. The role of the Holy Spirit is to bring us into union with the Lord Jesus, to keep us in that union, and to see that union flourish in communion with Him. Calvin makes this clear in his commentary on Psalm 133. He writes: "The peace that springs from Christ as the head, is diffused through the whole length and breadth of the Church."[32] The blessings that are in Christ flow over onto His body, the church, much as the anointing oil flowed over Aaron's head onto his beard and body. The anointing first comes on

30. Calvin, *Commentary on Romans*, 128, emphasis added. See also John Calvin, *The First Epistle of Paul the Apostle to the Corinthians*, ed. D. W. and T. F. Torrance, trans. J. W. Fraser (Grand Rapids: Eerdmans, 1960), 21.

31. See *Inst.* 2.16.19.

32. Calvin, *Commentary on the Book of Psalms*, 5.165.

the Lord Jesus Christ. Then the Holy Spirit gathers all the ingredients of that oil that flows over Christ and brings it to the body so that Christian believers who are regenerated may participate in Jesus Christ's graces.

For Calvin, the union with the Lord Jesus that comes through the Holy Spirit involves—as has already been noted—mortification and vivification. Both of these are twofold. Regeneration includes an internal and an external mortification, as well as an internal and external vivification. Just as we are united by the Spirit to a whole Christ, we are united as whole individuals. The Spirit works in us to conform us to the Lord Jesus, incarnate and resurrected. Mortification of sin takes place in the Christian life, but so does a mortification of the body in suffering and ultimately in death.

Vivification of our spirit is involved in regeneration, but this is not restricted to the "inner man." It ultimately has in view the vivification of the whole person in the resurrection, when the Lord Jesus will transform the Christian's body of lowliness from its state of humiliation to be like His body of glory. The Spirit does not unite us to Spirit so that in the end we may become disembodied spirit. Rather, He unites us to the Son of God incarnate in our flesh. The hallmark of the Spirit's work, therefore, is ongoing conformity to Christ crucified and raised, causing us to share His death in order to share His resurrection, to taste His suffering in order that we might also taste His glory. The Spirit implants the seed of this at the beginning of the Christian life and nourishes it to the end.[33]

Adoption

Calvin opens *Institutes* Book 3 with a striking comment on the importance of union with Christ. "We must understand that as long as Christ remains outside of us, and we are separated from him, all that he has suffered and done for the salvation of the human race remains useless and of no value to us."[34]

---

33. See *Inst.* 3.7–9.

34. *Inst.* 3.1.1.

Union with Christ becomes ours through faith. But, argues Calvin, we must go deeper than this in our analysis, for not all exercise faith. Thus, "reason itself teaches us to climb higher and to examine into the secret energy of the Spirit."[35]

This leads Calvin to a discussion of the titles of the Spirit. Here, he makes the remarkable statement that, in fact, "the first title" of the Holy Spirit is *Spirit of adoption*.[36] This title appears in the Scriptures only in Romans 8:15. In what sense, then, can it be "the first title"? It is first not in the sense of chronological but of theological priority.

The issue here transcends the question of whether Calvin is accurately assessing the biblical titles for the Spirit—for he is stressing that this is so within his own theology (of course because he believes this is true in Scripture).

This is the single most important description of the Spirit because, in Calvin's view, sonship is the most basic and comprehensive rubric for understanding the nature of the Christian life.[37] This is all of a piece with the fact that Calvin places strong emphasis on the gospel as the means by which we come to know the fatherhood of God, in which He brings us into His family and makes us His children. It is therefore something of a paradox that in some strands of the Reformed tradition believers have been discouraged from enjoying any assurance of their sonship. What good father in this world would want to bring his children up without the assurance that they are his children? Would the Father of lights (James 1:17) do that?

The model for all true fatherhood is rooted in the fatherhood of God. Calvin considers this truth to be a glorious liberation, in some senses his own parallel to Luther's appreciation of justification. The God of all glory not only becomes our Father, but wishes to assure His children that this is so. That is why Calvin says in *Institutes* 3.2.7 that

---

35. Ibid.

36. *Inst.* 3.1.3.

37. *Adoptio*—sonship—which Calvin frequently uses, serves virtually as the summary term for what it means to be a Christian. See *Institutes* 3.1.3; 3.2.22; 3.6.3; 3.11.6; 3.14.18; 3.17.6; 3.18.2; 3.20.36; 3.21.7; etc. Cf. also the discussion of God's Fatherhood in Brian A. Gerrish, *Grace and Gratitude* (Minneapolis: Fortress Press, 1993), 87–123.

we possess a right definition of faith only when we think of it as "a firm and certain knowledge of God's benevolence towards us."

This definition of faith has evoked considerable controversy, especially when contrasted with the emphasis of later Reformed writers that assurance is *not* of the essence of faith. But it should be remembered here that Calvin is defining faith; he is not describing the Christian life as, for example, the Westminster divines were to do.

For Calvin, faith in its essence is a joyful assurance. It is joyful because it has Jesus Christ in its sights and nothing else. But Calvin also recognizes that experience is not always identical to definition, as the rest of *Institutes* 3.2 demonstrates. We are living in the rough and tumble of an eschatological tension in which the Spirit has "already" united us to Christ but "not yet" consummated that work. Faith experiences the joy of the "already" but also tastes the struggles of the "not yet." Furthermore, life in the Spirit is lived out within the context of conflict with the flesh. The Spirit's ministry takes place not in a hermetically sealed laboratory where definitions of faith are written, but, as Calvin makes clear, in the nitty-gritty of the Christian life, where "the Spirit also helpeth our infirmities" (Rom. 8:26).

Communion

The adopted children of God have the witness of the Spirit of sonship and cry, "Abba Father" (Rom. 8:15). In their darkest moments, Christians cry out to their heavenly Father and experience this remarkable indication that they know themselves to belong to the Lord.[38]

But how does the Holy Spirit further enrich our lives within the context of our communion with Christ? Here it may be worth noting how the Lord's Supper ("the Communion service") fits into Calvin's theology as a whole.

In the aftermath of the painful split at the Marburg Colloquy between Luther and Ulrich Zwingli over the meaning of the Supper, Calvin argued that at the Lord's Supper the church does in fact have communion with Christ, but He is not located in the *res* (the actual things) of the Supper, the bread and the wine.

38. Calvin, *Commentary on Romans*, 167–71.

Calvin thus distances himself from both Rome and Luther in the way he understands the presence of Christ at the Lord's Supper. He denies the presence of Christ's humanity "in" the bread and the wine, since He has ascended to the right hand of the Father. Yet he does not want to withdraw into a "memorialist" doctrine in which all that is actually present is the believer's reflections on the death of His Savior.

Calvin admittedly describes that presence in ways that have disturbed some of the best Reformed theologians. He writes about the virtue or power that is communicated to us in the Lord's Supper being infused into ("poured into") us from the flesh and blood of Jesus Christ. This can easily strike readers as overly materialistic language.

The key to understanding Calvin's position is to remember the importance of the role of the Holy Spirit. All the resources for our blessing to which He has access are found in the incarnate, crucified, buried, raised, ascended, reigning, and returning Lord Jesus Christ. There are no other resources for the transformation of our lives because there is no mystical Christ, only the incarnate Christ. There is nothing else the Spirit can do, therefore, than bring us resources from the incarnate flesh of the Savior.

The Holy Spirit therefore brings us to receive from the real (i.e. the incarnate) Jesus:[39] "Christ's body is the only food to invigorate and enliven our soul."[40] There is no other Jesus. At the Lord's Supper, then, we have communion with Jesus in the Spirit, not communion with a spiritual Jesus.[41]

The role of the Holy Spirit, therefore, is to bring us to where the Lord Jesus is. He "closes the gap" in the space-time continuum between ourselves and Christ. This is the function of the *sursum corda* at the Lord's Supper: "Lift up your hearts" (to which we respond, "We lift them up to Thee, O Lord"). Calvin insists on this because true worship of and communion with Christ cannot be merely earthly

39. See, for example, *Inst.* 4.17.31.

40. *Inst.* 4.17.2.

41. "I am not satisfied with those persons who, recognizing that we have some communion with Christ, when they would show what it is, make us partakers of the Spirit only, omitting mention of flesh and blood." *Inst.* 4.17.7.

worship; it is heavenly worship, and is offered and experienced where Christ is, at the right hand of God.[42] By the ministry of the Spirit, we are lifted, as it were, to heaven, where we find the incarnate Christ and have communion with Him.

Calvin's teaching on the Supper is therefore integrated with his teaching on the work of the Holy Spirit, and is in turn embedded in his teaching about the person and work of the Lord Jesus. For it is on Christ the Spirit shines, and to Him we come by that same Spirit. Since everything we need is found in Him, it is into union and communion with Him that the Spirit brings us and keeps us.

This is why Calvin eloquently affirms:

> We see that our whole salvation and all its parts are comprehended in Christ [Acts 4:12]. We should therefore take care not to derive the least portion of it from anywhere else. If we seek salvation, we are taught by the very name of Jesus that it is "of him" [1 Cor. 1:30]. If we seek any other gifts of the Spirit, they will be found in his anointing. If we seek strength, it lies in his dominion; if purity, in his conception; if gentleness, it appears in his birth. For by his birth he was made like us in all respects [Heb. 2:17] that he might learn to feel our pain [Heb. 5:2]. If we seek redemption, it lies in his passion; if acquittal, in his condemnation; if remission of the curse, in his cross [Gal. 3:13]; if satisfaction, in his sacrifice; if purification, in his blood; if reconciliation, in his descent into hell; if mortification of the flesh, in his tomb; if newness of life, in his resurrection; if immortality, in the same; if inheritance of the heavenly kingdom, in his entrance into heaven; if protection, if security, if abundant supply of all blessings, in his Kingdom; if untroubled expectation of judgment, in the power given to him to judge. In short, since rich store of every kind of good abounds in him, let us drink our fill from this fountain and from no other.[43]

The Spirit then, as the bond of union between the Father and the Son, is also the bond of union between the Son and His people. It is

42. *Inst.* 4.17.36.
43. *Inst.* 2.16.19.

through His ministry that all that is in Christ for us becomes ours; indeed, Christ Himself "clothed in the gospel"[44] becomes ours.

The Spirit thus glorifies Christ, and in due season transforms us from one degree of glory to another. For "it is only under the guidance of the Spirit that we come into possession of Christ and all his benefits."[45]

In his remarkable vision for the unity of biblical theology, the being of God the Trinity, and the harmony of the three persons of the Trinity, Calvin portrays the Holy Spirit as the executive of the Godhead in bringing us into union and communion with Christ through illumination, regeneration, adoption, and communion. All this is ours through the Spirit alone. To the extent that Calvin grasped this and so eloquently expounded it as perhaps the supreme exponent of these truths, Warfield was surely saying no more than was warranted when he described the Genevan Reformer as, indeed, "the theologian of the Holy Spirit."

---

44. *Inst.* 3.2.6.

45. John Calvin, *The Second Epistle of Paul the Apostle to the Corinthians and the Epistles to Timothy, Titus and Philemon*, ed. D. W. and T. F. Torrance, trans. T. A. Smail (Grand Rapids: Eerdmans, 1964), 177.

III. Christian Living and Ministry

CHAPTER 6

Calvin the Revolutionary: Christian Living in a Fallen World

JOEL R. BEEKE AND RAY PENNINGS

"There were two Calvins: the statesman and the deeply religious man."[1]

— Guillaume Taylor

John Calvin's teaching has had a revolutionary impact. His influence has been cited as key to understanding the advance of capitalism,[2] democracy,[3] law,[4] and liberty,[5] to the point of his being called "the founder of America."[6] Michael Walzer said Calvinism transformed political thought by focusing on the actions of saints rather than princes, which then led to the modern understanding of citizenship. Calvin's view of individual conscience and vocation became the basis

1. Guillaume Taylor, St. Pierre Parish Council, Geneva, Switzerland, "Welcome and Announcements," at "Calvin500: A Quincentenary" (worship service held July 5, 2010, at St. Pierre Cathedral, Geneva).

2. Max Weber, *The Protestant Ethic and the Spirit of Capitalism* (New York: Charles Scribner's Sons, 1958).

3. Robert Kingdon, *Calvin and Calvinism: Sources of Democracy* (Lexington: D. C. Heath and Company, 1970).

4. John Witte Jr., *The Reformation of Rights: Law, Religion and Human Rights in Early Modern Calvinism* (Cambridge: Cambridge University Press, 2007).

5. Douglas Kelly, *The Emergence of Liberty in the Modern World* (Phillipsburg, N.J.: Presbyterian and Reformed, 1992).

6. This oft-repeated quote is attributed to German historian Leopold VanRanke (1795–1886); it is cited, among other places, in Doug Phillips, "John Calvin, Founding Father," *Washington Post* (July 7, 2009), available online at ht2tp://newsweek.washingtonpost.com/onfaith/guestvoices/2009/07/the_calvin_quincentenary_and_american_liberty.html

for "the literal reforming of human society, to the creation of a Holy Commonwealth in which conscientious activity would be encouraged and even required."[7] Those conclusions go beyond Calvin's ecclesiastical and theological influence, which was so significant that the historian Philip Schaff described Calvin as "one of the foremost leaders in the history of Christianity."[8]

Applying Calvin's revolutionary legacy to the early twenty-first century, however, has hardly been straightforward. In addition to critics who disagree with Calvin's theology or its implications, many of his theological heirs who seek his imprimatur for their approaches to Christian living differ from each other significantly in those approaches. Today, the few remnants of Constantinian assumptions about establishing a Christian society are disappearing. Orthodox believers are a distinct minority in our society and are on the fringes of cultural relevance. Whatever position one takes on the Calvinism that shaped our polities, few dispute that our political, social, and economic decision makers are quite ignorant of Calvinism's historical influence, and indifferent, if not openly hostile, to its continued influence. In that context, the question "How should we then live?"[9] takes on very different dimensions.

In this chapter, we cannot possibly cover the full details of a debate that has generated its own body of literature. Instead, we will consider the question "How should we then live?" in the context of a large corpus of secondary literature regarding Calvin and his influence, which has grown considerably with the commemoration of the five-hundredth anniversary of Calvin's birth on July 10, 2009. Much of this literature fits into two genres. One focuses on Calvin

---

7. Michael Walzer, "Calvinists Become Revolutionaries," in Kingdon, *Calvin and Calvinism*, 63.

8. Philip Schaff, "Calvin's Life and Labors," *Presbyterian Quarterly and Princeton Review* 4 (April 1875): 256.

9. The question is borrowed from the title of Francis Schaeffer's *How Should We Then Live? The Rise and Decline of Western Thought and Culture* (Old Tappan, N.J.: Fleming H. Revell, 1979), which is generally acknowledged to be a signature work in documenting the decline of Judeo-Christian morality as an underpinning of Western society.

the churchman and theologian, while the other focuses on Calvin the statesman or worldview thinker. The material lends itself to different emphases, audiences, and even styles of argument. But it also prompts a larger question. There was only one Calvin, and few would suggest that he was dualistic in his thinking. Rather, his thinking on personal piety and theology were never separate from his thinking on society. So how did Calvin's worldview—that the Christian faith has implications for society at large, economics, and politics—relate to his piety (which he defined as "that reverence joined with love of God which the knowledge of his benefits induces"[10]) and to his conception of practical, daily Christian living in a fallen world?

In the first part of this chapter, we will survey Calvin's worldview within the framework of four schools of contemporary Calvinist thinking. In the second section, we will summarize Calvin's thinking about piety and the Christian life. In the third, we will offer some conclusions that contribute to the present debate on how a revolutionary worldview and pietistic Christian living harmonize.

CALVIN'S WORLDVIEW PERSPECTIVE

The concept of worldview as it is formulated today would have been unfamiliar to Calvin. Using the word *worldview* to denote a comprehensive explanation of reality has become popular only in the past 150 years.[11] Since the time of the church fathers, people have debated how faith should be applied to questions involving ethics, the interpretation of the universe, and our place in it, but the Enlightenment changed the questions that were asked. In Calvin's time, the debates generally involved competing interpretations of faith and their applications to daily life. During the Enlightenment, religion increasingly was reduced to the private sphere. In the post-Enlightenment era, much of the debate turned to whether faith had

10. John Calvin, *Institutes of the Christian Religion*, ed. John T. McNeill, trans. Ford Lewis Battles (Philadelphia: Westminster Press, 1960), Book I, chapter 2, section 1. Hereafter the format *Inst.* 1.2.1 will be used.

11. David K. Naugle, *Worldview: The History of a Concept* (Grand Rapids: Eerdmans, 2002), 4.

anything meaningful to say regarding the world in which we live. A remedial concept of worldview developed in the post-Enlightenment church that promised a "fresh perspective on the holistic nature, cosmic dimensions, and universal application of the faith."[12]

Although the category of worldview is modern, the content of worldview understood from a biblical perspective is not. Rooted in an understanding of the sovereignty of God and His works of creation, providence, and redemption, the early church fathers debated the dominant philosophies of their time, attempting to provide the church with a framework within which to view life on this earth. In the second century, Irenaeus of Lyons refuted Gnosticism by initiating an alternative framework for understanding the world. In this, he relied heavily on the Genesis account.[13] Augustine's *City of God: Against the Pagans,* published in the fifth century, provided the earliest comprehensive worldview framework.[14] Among the Reformers, Calvin is most often cited as providing a clear and comprehensive worldview.[15] Calvin himself viewed his theological system as providing a "Christian philosophy."[16] The two "original worldview thinkers in Protestant evangelicalism" in the modern era were James Orr and Abraham Kuyper, whose views "flow from the theological wellsprings of the reformer of Geneva, John Calvin."[17] Today, various dimensions

---

12. Ibid., 5.

13. Irenaeus, "Against Heresies," available in *From Irenaeus to Grotius: A Sourcebook in Christian Political Thought*, ed. Oliver O'Donavan and Joan O'Donavan (Grand Rapids: Eerdmans, 1999).

14. Originally published as *De civitate Dei* (c. 425), available in "A Select Library of the Nicene and Post-Nicene Fathers of the Christian Church," ed. Philip Schaff, Vol. 2 (Grand Rapids, Eerdmans, 1978), accessed online at http://www.ccel.org/ccel/schaff/npnf102.i.html

15. In their *How Now Shall We Live*? (Wheaton: Tyndale, 1999), Charles Colson and Nancy Pearcy acknowledge that they stand on the shoulders of "especially John Calvin, Abraham Kuyper, C. S. Lewis, and Francis Schaeffer" (xiv). This book has been influential in contemporary evangelical and Reformed circles.

16. Naugle, *Worldview*, 5, note 4.

17. Ibid, 5. James Orr (1844–1913) was a Scottish Presbyterian theologian, apologist, minister, and educator whose most significant worldview book was *The*

of Calvin's worldview are disclosed in the appeals made to Calvin by different "schools" of Reformed thinking.[18]

In *The Institutes of the Christian Religion*, Calvin defined wisdom as "the knowledge of God and of ourselves,"[19] clearly stating that the purpose of life for all humans—"the law of their being"—is to "learn to know God."[20] Calvin's perspective on knowing God was not mystical or narrowly spiritual. Rather, he called readers to gaze upon God's perfections "in the whole structure of the universe," for He has been pleased to "daily place himself in our view, that we cannot open our eyes without being compelled to behold him."[21] He encouraged the careful study of astronomy, medicine, and the natural sciences, noting "that those who are more or less intimately acquainted with those liberal studies are thereby assisted and enabled to obtain a deeper insight into the secret workings of divine wisdom."[22] Calvin credited the "astonishing discoveries and inventing of so many wonderful arts" as "sure indications of the agency of God in man."[23] Failure to acknowledge the contribution made by men throughout history, including unbelievers, is ingratitude to God, he concluded.[24]

Affirming the world as God's world is a clear starting point for Calvin's worldview, but that viewpoint must be put into a proper relationship to Scripture if we are to understand Calvin rightly. Calvin

---

Christian View of God and the World as Centering in the Incarnation (Edinburgh: Andrew Eliot, 1893). Abraham Kuyper (1837–1920) was a Dutch theologian, minister, journalist, and politician whose book *Lectures on Calvinism* (Grand Rapids: Eerdmans, 1931), which provided the content of his 1898 Stone Lectures at Princeton University, is usually cited as his signature work.

18. We use the term *schools* in quotation marks since these groupings are ours and the extent to which those cited might self-identify with these groupings varies. Whereas "neo-Calvinism" and the "two-kingdom" perspective are more defined, what we have labeled "neo-Puritanism" and "Old Calvinism" are much looser categories.

19. *Inst.* 1.1.1.

20. *Inst.* 1.3.3.

21. *Inst.* 1.5.1.

22. *Inst.* 1.5.2.

23. *Inst.* 1.5.5.

24. *Inst.* 1.5.4.

wrote, "Therefore while it becomes man seriously to employ his eyes in considering the works of God since a place has been assigned him in this most glorious theatre that he may be a spectator of them, his special duty is to give ear to the Word, that he may the better profit."[25] Few would disagree with B. B. Warfield's summary:

> The Calvinist is the man who sees God: God in nature, God in history, God in grace. Everywhere he sees God in His mighty stepping, everywhere he feels the working of His mighty arm, the throbbing of His mighty heart. The Calvinist is the man who sees God behind all phenomena and in all that occurs recognizes the hand of God, working out His will. [The Calvinist] makes the attitude of the soul to God in prayer its permanent attitude in all its life activities; [he] casts himself on the grace of God alone, excluding every trace of dependence on self from the whole work of his salvation.[26]

Let us look now at four perspectives of contemporary Calvinistic thinking to see how they flesh out Calvin's worldview in practice. We will begin with the neo-Calvinist school of thought.

The Neo-Calvinist Perspective

Is seeing God everywhere a mandate to pursue Christian activity in every area of life? Kuyper thought so. In the Stone Lectures at Princeton in 1898, Kuyper described the Calvinist worldview and its logical consequences for Christians in words that have become a kind of mantra for neo-Calvinists:[27] "There is not a square inch in the whole domain of our human existence over which Christ, who

---

25. *Inst.* 1.6.2.

26. Benjamin B. Warfield, *Calvin as Theologian and Calvinism Today* (London: Evangelical Press, 1969), 23–24.

27. We use the term *neo-Calvinism* to refer to those who identify with Abraham Kuyper and his interpretation of Calvinism. The first known usage of the term *neo-Calvinism* has been ascribed to Free University of Amsterdam Professor A. Anema in an 1897 article. Cf. John Bolt, *A Free Church, A Holy Nation* (Grand Rapids: Eerdmans, 2001), 444, note 4.

is Sovereign over *all*, does not cry: 'Mine!'"[28] Taking his lead, neo-Calvinists have labored to create "Christian" organizations in almost every sphere, dedicated to implementing a "Christian philosophy" of all kinds of things. Kuyper understood Christianity as a life system that was totally at odds with non-Christian culture. Given the radically different presuppositions on which cultural activity was based, Kuyper emphasized the need to form distinctly Christian organizations.

The results of this view were radically different from the cultural activities pursued by unbelievers. As David Naugle notes:

> Regenerate people with a Christian worldview produce a roughly theistic interpretation of science, and non-regenerate people with a non-Christian worldview produce an idolatrous science. While Kuyper carefully nuances his position to avoid absurd conclusions, nonetheless he is clear that the experience of *palingenesis* [spiritual regeneration], which radically alters the content of human consciousness and reshapes worldview, makes a decisive difference in the way the cosmos is interpreted and science is pursued.[29]

Kuyper's approach has had far-reaching implications. According to Richard Niebuhr, the gospel should transform culture.[30] God created all things good; the Fall corrupted both man and creation, but the redemption of Jesus Christ is complete and, ultimately, all things will be redeemed. The kingdom of God extends to all spheres of life and "grace restores nature,"[31] even though we will have to wait until the Second Coming to see this fully realized.

---

28. Abraham Kuyper, "Sphere Sovereignty," in *Abraham Kuyper: A Centennial Reader*, ed. James D. Bratt (Grand Rapids: Eerdmans, 1998), 488.

29. David Naugle, "The Lordship of Christ Over the Whole of Life: An Introduction to the Thought of Abraham Kuyper," delivered at a symposium at Dallas Baptist University, February 2, 2001, and available online at http://www3.dbu.edu/naugle/pdf/abraham_kuyper.pdf, 8.

30. Richard Neibuhr, *Christ and Culture* (New York: Harper and Row, 1956).

31. Albert Wolters, *Creation Regained: Biblical Basics for a Reformational Worldview* (Carlisle, Cumbria, U.K.: Paternoster, 1996).

The Two-Kingdom Perspective

Advocates of a two-kingdom perspective, such as Daryl Hart, strongly disagree with Kuyper's call to reform every sphere of life. Rather than applying faith to every area of life because of a Calvinist worldview, they are convinced they must reform the church, which then will have a direct effect on economics, politics, and education. Their intent is first and foremost religious, and cultural transformation is a byproduct of church reform, Hart says.[32] Any attempts to create an integrated Christian system of thought on this side of eternity are thus foolish and distract the church from her central calling.[33] Though Scripture offers some principles that shed light on the public questions of our day, there is enough ambiguity that Christians will come to different conclusions on many current issues. Those with a two-kingdom perspective advocate an individual approach to social issues and warn against the danger of corporate activity.

Adherents of the two-kingdom perspective support their position by citing various passages in the *Institutes* in which Calvin uses two-kingdom language. Here is one prime example:

> Therefore, in order that none of us may stumble on that stone, let us first consider that there is a twofold government in man (*duplex esse in homine regimen*): one aspect is spiritual, whereby the conscience is instructed in piety and in reverencing God; the second is political, whereby man is educated for the duties of humanity and citizenship that must be maintained among men. These are usually called the "spiritual" and the "temporal" jurisdiction (not improper terms) by which is meant that the former sort of government pertains to the life of the soul, while the latter has to do with the concerns of the present life, not only with food and clothing but with laying down laws whereby a man may live his life among other men holily, honorably, and

32. D. G. Hart, "Creating a New Set of Sensibilities," in *Modern Reformation* 18, 4 (June-July 2009), 29–30.

33. D. G. Hart, "Christian Scholars, Secular Universities and the Problem of the Antithesis," in *Christian Scholars Review* 30 (2001): 383–402. See also Hart's *A Secular Faith: Why Christianity Favors the Separation of Church and State* (Chicago: Ivan R. Dee, 2006).

> temperately. For the former resides in the inner mind, while the latter regulates only outward behavior. The one we may call the spiritual kingdom, the other, the political kingdom. Now these two, as we have divided them, must always be examined separately; and while one is being considered, we must call away and turn aside the mind from thinking about the other. There are in man, so to speak, two worlds, over which different kings and different laws have authority.[34]

Two-kingdom advocates do not ascribe "Christian" to any opinion or intuition. Belief is personal, and believers are called to belong to a body of believers known as the Christian church. With a strong ecclesiology, often quoting Calvin's approval of Cyprian's saying, "You cannot have God as your Father if you do not have the church as your mother,"[35] two-kingdom adherents focus on the individual calling of believers to live faithfully as part of the body of Christ in the context of the community in which they find themselves.

The Neo-Puritan Perspective

With the rise of New Calvinists,[36] or neo-Puritans[37] (which is what we will call them to avoid confusion with the term *neo-Calvinists*), issues are being framed in a different manner. This movement is

---

34. *Inst.* 3.19.15.

35. *Inst.* 4.1.4.

36. With the term *New Calvinists*, we have in mind the movement documented in Collin Hansen's *Young, Restless, and Reformed: A Journalist's Journey with the New Calvinists* (Wheaton: Crossway, 2008). This label was applied by *Time* magazine, which, in March 2009, included New Calvinism as one of the "Ten ideas changing the world right now." Cf. http://www.time.com/time/specials/packages/article/0,28804,1884779_1884782_1884760,00.html

37. The term *neo-Puritan* has been variously used and claimed. Its most common usage seems to be by those objecting to religious-based arguments in the public square (cf. Ron Brandt, "Defending Public Education from the Neo-Puritans," *Educational Leadership* 44, 8 [May 1987]: 3). Those associated with the Theonomist and Reconstructionist movement in the early 1990s described themselves as neo-Puritans (Bolt, *A Free Church, A Holy Nation,* 307, note 17). We use the term loosely to describe those who adhere to an orthodox Calvinist soteriology (e.g., five-point Calvinists), are engaged with their cultural context, and place significant emphasis on personal piety and spiritual exercises.

characterized by a rediscovery of two doctrines: God's sovereignty and God's glory.[38] People in this movement come from a range of church backgrounds with varying ecclesiologies, including churches that make no pretence of being confessionally Reformed. But while neo-Puritanism is a disparate movement without coherence of thought on social engagement, its adherents still contribute to the discussion.

At least two things are emerging from the neo-Puritans: a political philosophy that is rooted in a love response to the challenges of our time and an emphasis on rediscovering transcendence, even in the mundane.

R. Albert Mohler Jr. suggests, "Love of neighbor for the sake of loving God is a profound political philosophy that strikes a balance between the disobedience of political disengagement and the idolatry of politics as our main priority."[39] Neo-Puritans believe that, in the midst of communities, Christians act as agents of salt and light to bring unbelieving neighbors into the kingdom of God. Mohler notes: "Love of neighbor grounded in our love for God requires us to work for good in the City of Man, even as we set as our first priority the preaching of the gospel, [which is] the only means of bringing citizens of the City of Man into citizenship of the city of God."[40] Cultural engagement is obedient service that brings glory to God, but it is also utilitarian in serving as a means of pre-evangelism.

It is not surprising that an approach based on loving one's neighbor has its priorities set by the issues of the day. Whether the issue is abortion, euthanasia, poverty, civil rights, or the environment, many arguments for personal engagement are based on empathy with victims. Typically, there are references to a worldview, reaching back through history to Calvin and Augustine, but the response this promotes is primarily diaconal. A common theme of neo-Puritan literature is establishing ministries of mercy that alleviate human suffering and provide the opportunity for the gospel to be preached.

---

38. Hansen, *Young, Restless, and Reformed,* 17.

39. R. Albert Mohler Jr., *Culture Shift: Engaging Current Issues with Timeless Truth* (Colorado Springs: Multnomah, 2008), 4.

40. Ibid., 3.

Neo-Puritanism tends to emphasize affections as well as intellect. John Piper writes: "My whole project theologically is to say that God is more God-centered than any other being in the universe, and then to back that up with dozens of texts that say God does everything for his glory. God is most glorified when we're most satisfied in him. Affections are central—not just marginal—and it's okay to be happy in God."[41]

This relates closely to a second emphasis on Christian social engagement in neo-Puritanism: rediscovering the transcendent in the midst of the mundane. In the introduction to Tullian Tchividjian's recent book *Unfashionable,* Tim Keller hears "ringing calls to form a distinct, 'thick' Christian counterculture as perhaps the ultimate witness to the presence of the future, the coming of the kingdom."[42] Tchividjian says this witness has less to do with political engagement or evangelistic strategies than with "living with the people we're trying to reach and showing them what human life and community look like when the gospel is believed and embraced."[43] It is demonstrated in two ways: first, by rejecting dominant cultural trends and living "unfashionably," and, second, by living as "transplants looking homeward" for a "new, sin-free physical world with new, sin-free physical bodies" with new, sin-free job responsibilities and personal relationships that believers one day will inherit. Tchividjian concludes, "The world desperately needs the church to be the church, reflecting the kingdom of God so that those who are lost will know where to turn when their own kingdoms begin to collapse."[44]

The Old Calvinist Perspective

A fourth approach may be called the "Old Calvinist" perspective. Although the term has been used as a pejorative by some in contrasting

---

41. John Piper, *Desiring God* (Sisters, Ore.: Multnomah, 1996), 15.

42. Timothy Keller, "Foreword," in Tullian Tchividjian, *Unfashionable: Making a Difference in the World by Being Different* (Colorado Springs: Multnomah, 2009), xvii.

43. Ibid., 112

44. Ibid., 78–79.

it with New Calvinism, we do not intend it as such. Rather, we are using the term to describe a category of orthodox Reformed voices who at various times over the past century have responded to what they perceive as excesses or errors in the way the church has engaged culture, and have warned against these excesses as compromising the "old paths." While rarely advocating total withdrawal from the culture, the message of these voices appears to be withdrawal or disengagement, given that they see the engagement that prompted their response as dangerous.[45]

At various times in the past century, many of these Old Calvinists have warned that the social engagements they were observing were harmful to the church. They based these convictions not only on Scripture's call to "love not the world nor the things of the world" (1 John 2:15), but also on the teachings of Calvin. Calvin often implied that cultural engagement can lead to worldliness, and that when the church attempts to influence the culture, the culture is usually more effective at influencing the church.

For example, Calvin said, "As soon as the least ray of hope beams upon us, from the world, we are torn away from the Lord, and alienated from the pursuit of the heavenly life."[46] Again, "The Lord calls all his people, as by the sound of the trumpet, to be wanderers, lest they should become fixed in their nests on earth."[47] That led him to conclude: "The only way to walk through life happily is to walk holily and harmlessly in the world, in the service and fear of God."[48]

Consider the political order, Calvin said. Since this world is fallen and liable to the wrath of God, the political order is one way for God to express His wrath, despite His own establishment of the state as an instrument to sustain order in the world. If we as citizens are placed under a harsh ruler, we should remind ourselves that worldly kings are established by heaven, and that, because of our own wickedness, we

---

45. Cf. "New Calvinism vs. Old Calvinism," http://theresurgence.com/new_calvinism.

46. *Commentary* on Genesis 48:3.

47. *Commentary* on Genesis 47:8.

48. *Inst.* 3.9.2.

deserve even worse than we have received.[49] If, however, we are placed under good and helpful leaders, we ought to be grateful for God's providential care. A just and good magistrate is a rare gift granted to few. Those who receive this gift should pray for their leaders and cultivate life in the fear of God. They should give thanks to God for a peaceable life in this world.[50]

John MacArthur, who in this regard takes the Old Calvinist position, cites four arguments against political activism on the part of Christians. He says political activism (1) denigrates the sovereignty of God over human history and events, (2) uses fleshly and selfish means to promote biblical values, (3) creates a false sense of morality, and (4) risks alienating unbelievers by viewing them as political enemies rather than a mission field. MacArthur concludes: "I believe America's heart can be turned toward God, but only through the power of the Spirit, one person at a time. And you and I have at our disposal the only means to bring genuine, lasting change: God's good news of salvation. So use it for the glory of God's kingdom."[51] Promoting godly living and the fruits of the Spirit is a mission "far more good and profitable to men than any amount of social and political activism.... [Christians] are content very much to let the worldly people deal with the worldly things of this world."[52]

Sometimes categories exaggerate differences or widen gulfs; that is not our intent here. What is clear is that conservative churches that view themselves as heirs of Calvin's legacy vary greatly in their view of Calvin as a cultural revolutionary and how his teachings should be applied today. Some of these differences are due to different interpretations of various aspects of Calvin's thought, but many of them stem from practical questions that confront us today in our fallen world, such as: How do we integrate a biblical worldview with

---

49. *Commentary* on Exodus 3:16–17.

50. *Inst.* 2.8.37; cf. Sang Jo Kim, "Accept Sorrow and Accept Comfort: An Understanding of Calvin's Political Perspective" (unpublished paper, Puritan Reformed Theological Seminary, April 2009), 4–5, 29.

51. John MacArthur, *Why Government Can't Save You: An Alternative to Political Activism* (Nashville: Word, 2000), 192.

52. Ibid., 145, 153.

a close walk with God? How do we maintain biblical priorities in a fallen world while seeking to reform human society?

To help answer such questions, let us undertake a brief survey of Calvin's view of piety.

CALVIN'S COMPREHENSIVE PIETY AND CHRISTIAN LIVING

Pietas was a major theme of Calvin's theology. As John T. McNeill says, Calvin's theology is "piety described at length."[53] Calvin was determined to confine theology within the limits of piety.[54] In his prefatory address to King Francis I in the *Institutes*, Calvin said he wrote the book "solely to transmit certain rudiments by which those who are touched with any zeal for religion might be shaped to true godliness [*pietas*]."[55]

The term *pietas* for Calvin is wholly positive and has none of the sense of disengagement and withdrawal from life and theology that the pejorative use can have in English. Calvin viewed *pietas* as the right attitude of man toward God. Piety includes true knowledge, heartfelt worship, saving faith, filial fear, prayerful submission, and reverential love.[56] Knowing who and what God is (theology) involves right attitudes toward God and doing what He wants (piety). In his first catechism,

53. Cited in John Hesselink, "The Development and Purpose of Calvin's Institutes," in *Articles on Calvin and Calvinism, Vol. 4, Influences upon Calvin and Discussion of the 1559 Institutes,* ed. Richard C. Gamble (New York: Garland, 1992), 215–16. Parts of this section have been adapted from Joel R. Beeke, "The Piety of Calvin," in *The Cambridge Companion to John Calvin,* ed. Donald K. McKim (Cambridge: University Press, 2004), 125–52.

54. See Brian A. Gerrish, "Theology within the Limits of Piety Alone: Schleiermacher and Calvin's Doctrine of God" (1981), reprinted in Brian A. Gerrish, *The Old Protestantism and the New* (Chicago: University of Chicago Press, 1982), chap. 12.

55. "Prefatory address to King Francis I of France," *Inst.* 1:9.

56. Cf. Lucien Joseph Richard, *The Spirituality of John Calvin* (Atlanta: John Knox Press, 1974), 100–101; Sou-Young Lee, "Calvin's Understanding of *Pietas*," in *Calvinus Sincerioris Religionis Vindex*, ed. W. H. Neuser and B. G. Armstrong (Kirksville, Mo.: Sixteenth Century Studies, 1997), 226–33; H. W. Simpson, "*Pietas* in the *Institutes* of Calvin," in *Reformational Tradition: A Rich Heritage and*

Calvin wrote, "True piety consists in a sincere feeling which loves God as Father as much as it fears and reverences him as Lord, embraces his righteousness, and dreads offending him worse than death."[57] In the *Institutes,* Calvin was more succinct: "I call 'piety' that reverence joined with love of God which the knowledge of his benefits induces."[58] Love and reverence for God are integrally linked to any knowledge of Him, and embrace all of life. As Calvin said, "The whole life of Christians ought to be a sort of practice of godliness."[59] Or, as the first subtitle of the *Institutes* stated, "Embracing almost the whole sum of piety & whatever is necessary to know of the doctrine of salvation: A work most worthy to be read by all persons zealous for piety."[60]

The goal of piety, as well as that of the entire Christian life, is to glorify God. The glory of God shines in His attributes, in the structure of the world, and in the death and resurrection of Jesus Christ.[61] Glorifying God supersedes personal salvation for a truly pious person.[62] Calvin thus wrote to Cardinal Sadoleto: "It is not very sound theology to confine a man's thought so much to himself, and not to set before

Lasting Vocation (Potchefstroom: Potchefstroom University for Christian Higher Education, 1984), 179–91.

57. *John Calvin: Catechism 1538*, ed. and trans. Ford Lewis Battles (Pittsburgh: Pittsburgh Theological Seminary), 2.

58. *Inst.* 1.2.1.

59. *Inst.* 3.19.2.

60. *Institutes of the Christian Religion: 1536 Edition,* trans. Ford Lewis Battles, rev. ed. (Grand Rapids: Eerdmans, 1986). The original Latin title reads: *Christianae religionis institutio total fere pietatis summam et quidquid est in doctrina salutis cognitu necessarium complectens, omnibut pietatis studiosis lectu dignissimum opus ac recens editum* (*Joannis Calvini opera selecta,* ed. Peter Barth, Wilhelm Niesel, and Dora Scheuner, 5 vols. [Munich: Chr. Kaiser, 1926–52], 1:19 [hereafter, *OS*]). From 1539 on, the title was simply *Institutio Christianae Religionis*, but "zeal for piety" continued to be a great goal of Calvin's work. See Richard A. Muller, *The Unaccommodated Calvin: Studies in the Foundation of a Theological Tradition* (New York: Oxford University Press, 2000), 106–107.

61. *Inst.* 3.2.1; Calvin, *Ioannis Calvini opera quae supersunt omnia,* ed. Wilhelm Baum, Edward Cunitz, and Edward Reuss, *Corpus Reformatorum,* vols. 29–87 (Brunsvigae: C.A. Schwetschke and Son, 1863–1900), 43:428; 47:316. Hereafter, *CO.*

62. *CO* 26:693.

him, as the prime motive for his existence, zeal to illustrate the glory of God.... I am persuaded that there is no man imbued with true piety who will not consider as insipid that long and labored exhortation to zeal for heavenly life, a zeal which keeps a man entirely devoted to himself and does not, even by one expression, arouse him to sanctify the name of God."[63]

Glorifying God is the purpose for which we were created, so the goal of the regenerate is to live out the purpose of his original creation.[64] The pious man, according to Calvin, confesses: "We are God's: let us therefore live for him and die for him. We are God's: let his wisdom and will therefore rule all our actions. We are God's: let all the parts of our life accordingly strive toward him as our only lawful goal."[65]

How do we glorify God? Calvin's answer was this: "God has prescribed for us a way in which he will be glorified by us, namely, piety, which consists in the obedience of his Word. He that exceeds these bounds does not go about to honor God, but rather to dishonor him."[66] Obedience to God's Word means taking refuge in Christ for forgiveness of our sins, knowing Him through His Word, serving Him with a loving heart, doing good works in gratitude for His goodness, and exercising self-denial to the point of loving our enemies.[67] This response involves total surrender to God, His Word, and His will.[68] Calvin thus famously said, "I offer thee my heart, Lord, promptly and sincerely." That desire can be realized only through communion with Christ and participation in Him, for outside of Christ even the most religious person lives for himself. Only in Christ can the pious live as willing servants of their Lord, faithful soldiers of their Commander, and obedient children of their Father.[69]

For Calvin, then, piety is comprehensive theologically, ecclesiastically, and practically. Theologically, mystical union with Christ is

63. *OS* 1:363–64.
64. *CO* 24:362.
65. *Inst.* 3.7.1.
66. *CO* 49:51.
67. *CO* 26:166; 33:186; 47:377–78; 49:245; 51:21.
68. *CO* 6:9–10.
69. *CO* 26:439–40.

the starting point for Christian living.[70] Such union is possible because Christ took on our human nature, filling it with His sinless virtue. If Christ had died and risen but had not applied His salvation to believers for their regeneration and sanctification, His work would have been ineffectual. Our piety shows that the Spirit of Christ is working in us what already has been accomplished in Christ. Christ administers His sanctification to the church through His royal priesthood so that the church may live piously for Him.[71]

Eccelesiastically, Calvin understood spiritual growth to occur within the context of the church. The church is mother, educator, and nourisher of every believer, Calvin said, for the Holy Spirit acts in her. Believers cultivate piety by the Spirit through the church's teaching, progressing from spiritual infancy to adolescence to full manhood in Christ. They do not graduate from the church until they die.[72] This lifelong education in the read and preached Word, the administration of the sacraments, corporate prayer, and psalm-singing is offered in an atmosphere of genuine piety in which believers love and care for one another under the headship of Christ.[73] Growth in piety is impossible apart from the church, for piety is fostered by the communion of saints. The community constrains believers to borrow from each other's gifts, thereby encouraging the growth of their gifts and love.[74] Within the church, believers "cleave to each other in the mutual distribution of gifts."[75] Each member has his own place and gifts to use within the body.[76] Ideally, the church uses these gifts in symmetry and proportion, ever reforming and growing toward perfection.[77]

It is important to note that the categories of "private" and "public" as we understand them were foreign to Calvin's day. The notion of an

70. Howard G. Hageman, "Reformed Spirituality," in *Protestant Spiritual Traditions,* ed. Frank C. Senn (New York: Paulist Press, 1986), 61.

71. *Inst.* 2.16.16.

72. *Inst.* 4.1.4–5.

73. *Commentary* on Psalm 20:10.

74. *Commentary* on Romans 12:6.

75. *Commentary* on 1 Corinthians 12:12.

76. *Commentary* on 1 Corinthians 4:7.

77. *Commentary* on Ephesians 4:12.

individual existing on his own, free to exercise voluntarism by joining and then leaving the church as desired, would have seemed nonsensical. Union with Christ meant union with the body of Christ. The health of the whole church affected the parts, just as the health of the part affected the whole. So the church was the nursery of piety, but personal piety was also required. The Christian strives for piety because he loves righteousness, longs to live to God's glory, and delights to obey God's rule of righteousness set forth in Scripture.[78] God Himself is the focal point of the Christian life,[79] which therefore is characterized by self-denial expressed in Christ-like cross-bearing.[80]

For Calvin, such piety "is the beginning, middle, and end of Christian living."[81] Book III, Sections 6–10, of the *Institutes* provides a useful summary of Calvin's thought on living piously in a fallen world.[82] Six elements are involved.

Prayer

Prayer is the chief element of piety, Calvin said.[83] Prayer evidences God's grace to the believer even as the believer offers praises to God and asks for His faithfulness. It communicates piety both privately and corporately.[84]

---

78. *Inst.* 3.6.2.

79. *Inst.* 3.6.3.

80. *Inst.* 3.7–8.

81. *Commentary* on 1 Timothy 4:7–8.

82. This section was first translated into English in 1549 as *The Life and Conversation of a Christian Man* and has been reprinted often as *The Golden Booklet of the True Christian Life.*

83. See R. D. Loggie, "Chief Exercise of Faith: An Exposition of Calvin's Doctrine of Prayer," *Hartford Quarterly* 5 (1965): 65–81; H. W. Maurer, "An Examination of Form and Content in John Calvin's Prayers" (Ph.D. dissertation, Edinburgh, 1960).

84. Due to space limitations, prayer is considered here in its personal dimension, but for Calvin, prayer was also of vast importance in its communal aspect. See Elsie McKee for a selection of individual and family prayers Calvin prepared as patterns for Genevan children, adults, and households, as well as a number of prayers from his sermons and biblical lectures (Elsie McKee, ed., *John Calvin: Writings on Pastoral Piety* [Mahwah, N.J.: Paulist Press, 2001]). Cf.

Calvin addressed the objection that prayer seems superfluous in light of God's omniscience and omnipotence, noting that God ordains prayer as an exercise of piety more for man than for Himself. Providence must be understood in the sense that God ordains the means along with the ends, Calvin said. Prayer is thus a means to receive what God has planned to bestow,[85] a way in which believers seek out and receive what God has determined to do for them from eternity.[86]

Repentance

Calvin saw repentance as a lifelong process. It is not merely the start of the Christian life; it *is* the Christian life, he said. Repentance is the lifelong response of the believer to the gospel in outward behavior, mind, heart, attitude, and will.[87] It begins with the heart turning to God and proceeds from a pure, earnest fear of Him. It involves dying to self and sin (mortification) and coming alive to righteousness (vivification) in Christ.[88] Calvin did not limit repentance to inward grace but viewed it as the redirection of a person's entire being to righteousness. Without pure, earnest fear of God, a person will not be aware of the heinousness of sin or want to die to it. Mortification is essential because, though sin ceases to reign in the believer, it does not cease to dwell in him.

Repentance is also characterized by newness of life. It involves growth in holiness as well as confession of sin. Mortification is the means to vivification, which Calvin defined as "the desire to live in a holy and devoted manner, a desire arising from rebirth; as if it were

---

Thomas A. Lambert, "Preaching, Praying, and Policing the Reform in Sixteenth Century Geneva" (Ph.D. dissertation, University of Wisconsin-Madison, 1998), 393–480; Joel R. Beeke, "The Communion of Men with God," in *John Calvin: A Heart for Devotion, Doctrine, and Doxology,* ed. Burk Parsons (Orlando, Fla.: Reformation Trust, 2008), 231–46.

85. *Inst.* 3.20.3.

86. Charles Partee, "Prayer as the Practice of Predestination," in *Calvinus Servus Christi*, ed. Wilhelm H. Neuser (Budapest: Pressabteilung des Raday-Kollegiums, 1988), 254.

87. *Inst.* 3.3.1–2, 6, 18, 20.

88. *Inst.* 3.3.5, 9.

said that man dies to himself that he may begin to live to God."[89] True self-denial results in a life devoted to justice and mercy. The pious both "cease to do evil" and "learn to do well." The words Calvin used to describe the pious Christian life (*reparatio*, *reformatio*, *renovatio*, *restitutio*) refer to our original state of righteousness. They indicate that a life of *pietas* is restorative in nature. Through Spirit-worked repentance, believers are restored to the image of God.[90]

Self-denial

The fruit of the believer's union with Jesus Christ is self-denial, which is the sacrificial dimension of piety. Self-denial includes the realization that we are not our own but belong to God. We live and die unto Him, according to the rule of His Word. Thus, self-denial is not self-centered, as was often the case in medieval monasticism, but God-centered.[91] Our greatest enemy is neither the devil nor the world, but ourselves. Self-denial also ignites the desire to seek the things of the Lord throughout our lives. It leaves no room for pride, lasciviousness, or worldliness. It is the opposite of self-love because it is love for God.[92]

Self-denial involves the commitment to yield ourselves and everything we own to God as a living sacrifice. We then are prepared to love others and to esteem them better than ourselves, not by viewing them as they are in themselves, but by viewing the image of God in them. This uproots our love of strife and self, and replaces it with a spirit of gentleness and helpfulness.[93] Our love for others then flows from the heart, and the only limit to helping them is the extent of our resources.[94]

---

89. *Inst.* 3.3.3; Randall C. Gleason, *John Calvin and John Owen on Mortification: A Comparative Study in Reformed Spirituality* (New York: Peter Lang, 1995), 61.

90. John H. Leith, *John Calvin's Doctrine of the Christian Life* (Louisville: Westminster/John Knox, 1989), 70–74.

91. *Inst.* 3.7.1.

92. *Inst.* 3.7.2.

93. *Inst.* 3.7.4–5.

94. *Inst.* 3.7.7; Merwyn S. Johnson, "Calvin's Ethical Legacy," in *The Legacy of John Calvin,* ed. David Foxgrover (Grand Rapids: CRC, 2000), 74.

Scripture's promises about the future consummation of the kingdom of God encourage us to persevere in self-denial. Such promises help us overcome obstacles that oppose self-renunciation and to bear adversity.[95] They also help us find true happiness because they help us do what we were created to do: love God above all and our neighbors as ourselves. Happiness is the result of the restoration of that love. Without self-denial, Calvin said, we may possess everything without possessing one particle of real happiness.

Cross-bearing

While self-denial focuses on inward conformity to Christ, cross-bearing centers on outward Christlikeness. Those who are in fellowship with Christ must prepare for a hard, toilsome life filled with many kinds of evil, Calvin said. This is due in part to sin's effect on our fallen world, but also to the believer's union with Christ. Because Christ's life was a perpetual cross, ours also must include suffering.[96] We not only participate in the benefits of Christ's atoning work on the cross, we experience the Spirit's work of transforming us into the image of Christ.[97]

Cross-bearing tests piety, Calvin said. Through cross-bearing, we are roused to hope, trained in patience, instructed in obedience, and chastened in pride. Cross-bearing is our medicine and our chastisement; it reveals the feebleness of our flesh and teaches us to suffer for the sake of righteousness.[98] Happily, God promises to be with us in all our sufferings. He even transforms suffering associated with persecution into comfort and blessing.[99]

The Present and Future Life

Through cross-bearing, we learn contempt for this present life when compared to the blessings of heaven. This life is nothing compared to

95. *Inst.* 3.7.8–10.

96. Richard C. Gamble, "Calvin and Sixteenth-Century Spirituality," in *Calvin Studies Society Papers,* ed. David Foxgrover (Grand Rapids: CRC, 1998), 34–35.

97. *Inst.* 3.8.1–2.

98. *Inst.* 3.8.3–9.

99. *Inst.* 3.8.7–8.

what is to come; life on earth is like smoke or a shadow. "If heaven is our homeland, what else is the earth but our place of exile? If departure from the world is entry into life, what else is the world but a sepulcher?" Calvin asked.[100] "No one has made progress in the school of Christ who does not joyfully await the day of death and final resurrection," he concluded.[101]

When explaining the Christian's relation to this world, Calvin defined opposites to find a middle way between them. Thus, on the one hand, cross-bearing crucifies us to the world and the world to us. On the other hand, the devout Christian enjoys this present life, albeit with due restraint and moderation, for he is taught to use things in this world for the purpose for which God intended them. Calvin was no ascetic; he enjoyed good literature, good food, and the beauties of nature. But he rejected all forms of earthly excess. He said the believer is called to Christlike moderation, which includes modesty, prudence, avoidance of display, and contentment with our lot,[102] for the hope of the life to come gives purpose to and enjoyment in our present life. This life is always straining after a better, heavenly life.[103]

Calvin offered four guidelines to help believers reach this balance: First, recognize that God is the giver of every good and perfect gift. This should restrain our lusts, because gratitude to God for His gifts cannot be expressed by greedy reception of them. Second, understand that if we have few possessions, we must bear poverty patiently lest we be ensnared by inordinate desire. Third, remember that we are stewards of the world in which God has placed us. Soon we will have to give an account to Him of our stewardship. Fourth, know that God has called us to Himself and to His service. Because of that calling, we strive to fulfill our tasks in His service, for His glory, and under His watchful, benevolent eye.[104]

100. *Inst.* 3.9.4.

101. *Inst.* 3.9.5.

102. Ronald S. Wallace, *Calvin's Doctrine of the Christian Life* (Edinburgh: Oliver and Boyd, 1959), 170–95.

103. *Inst.* 3.9.3.

104. *Inst.* 3.10.

Obedience

Unconditional obedience to God's will is the essence of piety, Calvin said. Piety links love, freedom, and discipline by subjecting all to the will and Word of God.[105] Love is the overarching principle that prevents piety from degenerating into legalism. At the same time, law provides the content for love.

Piety includes rules that govern the believer's response to all of life. Privately, those rules take the form of self-denial and cross-bearing; publicly, they are expressed in the exercise of church discipline, as Calvin implemented it in Geneva. In either case, the glory of God compels disciplined obedience. For Calvin, the pious Christian is neither weak nor passive in submitting to God's will but dynamically active in the pursuit of obedience, much like a distance runner, a diligent scholar, or a heroic warrior.[106]

Let us summarize Calvin's teaching on piety and Christian living in reference to the debate on engaging culture. Consider these seven points that are clearly evident in Calvin's teaching:

1. Calvin understood cultural engagement in the context of a believer's personal relationship with God; it flows out of that relationship and never exists independent of it. That is to say, the indicative precedes the imperative, not only in our practice but also in the articulation of our public theology.

2. Calvin discussed the Christian life comprehensively. He did not divide the natural world from the spiritual world in terms of Christian obedience, but assumed engagement in "all of life." In Calvin's spirituality, natural things became spiritual. Theologically, ecclesiastically, and practically, he strove to live what he taught.

3. A believer's relationship to God is the highest priority. Calvin warned against worldliness and falling into temptation. He said that keeping an unspoiled conscience and maintaining spiritual disciplines were a higher priority than social engagement.

---

105. Lionel Greve, "Freedom and Discipline in the Theology of John Calvin, William Perkins, and John Wesley: An Examination of the Origin and Nature of Pietism" (Ph.D. dissertation, The Hartford Seminary Foundation, 1976), 20.

106. Leith, *John Calvin's Doctrine of the Christian Life*, 82–86.

4. The institutional church plays a central role in a believer's spiritual growth. The church has preeminence over any other social institution, but it is preeminent in importance, not in hierarchical authority.

5. Life itself as well as social engagement results in cross-bearing. Calvin viewed crosses not only as problems to be overcome but also as God's providence to teach believers necessary lessons and draw them closer to Him.

6. Although the world is fallen and under divine punishment, God's providence prevents it from falling into utter chaos. Since the world still has remnants of good, the Christian should strive for its betterment.

7. We must look at time and the issues of the day in the context of eternity and in anticipation of future glory.

CONTEMPORARY IMPLICATIONS

Our intent is not to interject Calvin into a modern discussion and assign him to a particular school of thought. All of the schools previously mentioned pick up on themes present in Calvin's thought. How Calvin would have applied his thinking—which had revolutionary impact in his day—to the questions of our day is primarily an academic question. Part of the problem is that we are dealing in a post-Cartesian mode of discussion, where the evidence and tools of debate used in academic, social, and political discussions are vastly different from those of Calvin's time. Gerald Bilkes reminds us: "The Cartesian revolution prized knowledge that could be empirically verified, and under this new definition of science, piety was not welcome."[107] Calvin used the debating methods of his days to explain how Christians are to live in a fallen world.

The difficulty is that, at times, two Calvins appear to be involved in our debate. The neo-Calvinist says the fundamental presuppositions underlying the debate need to be changed if we are to have meaningful engagement. The two-kingdom perspective responds that that won't

107. Gerald Bilkes, "Heart-Reading: Recovering a Spiritual Approach to the Bible," *Puritan Reformed Journal* 1, 2 (2009): 14.

happen; when we try to engage in discussion, we end up calling things Christian that really aren't, resulting in pride and a misrepresentation of the gospel. The neo-Puritan says that that is why we should avoid a systemic approach; we should focus more on the individual needs of our neighbors and show them in ministries of mercy and by positive examples that faith makes a difference. The Old Calvinist says that in all of this activity, we are losing our focus and getting dirty as we dig around in the garbage cans of culture to retrieve a penny or two of value from the bottom. We and our culture need heart surgery, not Band-Aids.

The overlapping themes that emerge from Calvin's writings (covering material that we usually consider in literature of very different genres) help us apply Calvin's legacy to our culture today. Rather than attempting prescriptively to apply these themes to the four categories of cultural engagement that we outlined earlier or to create a new category—all of which requires more space than we have—we will simply enumerate three of the themes.

First, the overriding theme of Calvin's thought is the glory of God. The supreme purpose of knowledge and piety is not to achieve something great, such as the discovery of creation's potential or even the salvation of a man's soul. All of that is secondary to the glory of God, who is the substance of all things. This God-centeredness reminds us of the psalmist, who cites his inspiration for seeking out the works of God (Ps. 145). Although the imperfection of the saints means that the works they do often have destructive effects (as do the works of God in nature after the Fall—for example, hurricanes and tornadoes), that destruction does not give us reason to deny the hand of God in history or to cease to admire His glory. Our theology teaches us to expect tension between "the now and the not yet." The God-glorifying aspects of both the now and the not yet were Calvin's focus, and ought to be ours as well.

A second theme that emerges in Calvin's teachings is eschatological hope. God's purposes, even when revealed in time, direct us to their full achievement in eternity. The refiner's fire (1 Peter 3:10) will burn off the dross so radically that the purified gold will be beyond our recognition; its beauty will transcend our greatest expectations. Thus, our actions on earth are tangible reminders of the expectation that awaits the child of God. Herman Bavinck said it well:

> The substance of the city of God is present in this creation. Just as the caterpillar becomes a butterfly, as carbon is converted into diamond, as the grain of wheat upon dying in the ground produces other grains of wheat, as all of nature revives in the spring, dresses up in celebrative clothing, as the believing community is formed out of Adam's fallen race, as the resurrection body is raised from the body that is dead and buried in the earth, so too by the recreating power of Christ the new heaven and the new earth will one day emerge from the fire-purged elements of this world, radiating an enduring glory and forever set free from the bondage of decay. More glorious than this beautiful earth, more glorious than the earthly Jerusalem, more glorious even than Paradise will be the glory of the new Jerusalem whose architect and builder is God himself. The state of glory will be no mere restoration of the state of nature but a reformation which, thanks to the power of Christ, transforms all matter into form, all potency into actuality, and presents the entire creation before the face of God brilliant in unfading splendor and blossoming in a springtime of eternal youth.[108]

We also might note here that much of the worldview literature today uses the threefold categorization of (1) creation, (2) Fall, and (3) redemption. It might be more helpful for our discussion to return to the fourfold categorization of previous eras: (1) creation, (2) Fall, (3) salvation in time, and (4) restoration in eternity. While the same theological content can be contained in either set of categories, since redemption is for eternity, the benefit of the fourfold categorization is that it directs our attention more specifically to the biblical data regarding judgment, which too often is underemphasized in our day. The fourfold categorization forces us to consider the reality of God's punishment of sin, providing us incentive for holiness in our day and impressing us with the urgency of sharing the gospel with unbelievers. Also, it reminds us of the fullness of the redemption wrought by Christ

---

108. Herman Bavinck, *Reformed Dogmatics* (Grand Rapids: Baker Academic, 2008), 4:720.

Jesus, encouraging the believer, as the Heidelberg Catechism says, that "in body and soul, in life and death, I am not my own but belong to my faithful Savior Jesus Christ."[109] That reminder encourages us to serve the Lord in every sphere of life.

A third observation comes from the very exercise of examining our categories. It is easy for us to deal with issues in categories, and there is nothing wrong with this. Calvin was an excellent systematician and certainly dealt in categories. Yet, sometimes after we have divided a subject into parts, we deal with each part individually. Then, when we attempt to reconstitute the whole as the sum of those parts, we come up with a conclusion such as: there were two Calvins, the churchman and the statesman. Although Calvin dealt with material in categories to help us understand it, his thinking was integrated. He did not separate the individual believer from the church, loving God from loving one's neighbor, or God's command to serve Him with the soul as well as the body. They are all one in his teaching. Guillaume Taylor's statement at the head of the chapter is fundamentally flawed.

Calvin's worldview has an impregnable unity. There is no sacred and secular divide in his thinking, though he does give some priority to such callings and activities as preaching and worship. But according to Calvin, all Christians are to glorify Christ in every aspect of their lives. There is a biblical mandate for artistic endeavor, provided that such efforts distance themselves from sinful worldliness. Even as we long for the world to come, we are to value this life and the world, and not simply regard it as a waiting room for the Second Coming.

This unity of thought offers us valuable lessons for today. Our doctrine, piety, and worldview are not separate categories but integrated, the one shaping the other. The church is not a private institution, serving simply as a refueling station to energize its members to engage with this world or as a shelter to hide them from their obligations. The church is the bride of Christ, who is preparing for the bridegroom's great return. How must she prepare herself? She must get ready by

---

109. *Heidelberg Catechism*, Lord's Day 1, in *Doctrinal Standards, Liturgy, and Church Order,* ed. Joel R. Beeke (Grand Rapids: Reformation Heritage Books, 1999), 27.

proclaiming sound doctrine and boldly, without shame, speaking the truth about her beloved; by adorning herself with holiness so that she is an example of all the riches of grace from the One who has adorned her with His own righteousness; by reaching out in love to demonstrate that the love of God and love of neighbor are inseparable; and by waiting with anticipation until her bridegroom comes again.

Calvin's comprehensive piety was revolutionary in his day. He helped Christians across Europe to understand piety in terms of living every day in every part of life according to God's will and for His glory (Rom. 12:1–2). Through Calvin's influence, Reformed spirituality focused on how to live the Christian life in the family, the fields, the workshop, and the marketplace. This spirituality, in turn, was fleshed out by the Puritans, who became even more intense than Calvin in teaching how to live wholly to God in every area of life every minute of every day.

CHAPTER 7

Calvin and Preaching: The Power of the Word

JOEL R. BEEKE

John Calvin had a high view of preaching. He said preaching is "the most excellent of all things"[1] commended by God, and it must be held in the highest esteem among men. According to Calvin, preaching is not only a lofty calling, it is also powerful—not in a merely impressive or affecting way through undiscerning and empty shows of rhetoric, but by the anointing ministry of the Holy Spirit, which alone is truly powerful. This is the kind of preaching that all times require.

Calvin taught that by the Holy Spirit's grace, nothing in the world is as powerful as the preached Word of God. The words *power* and *powerful* refer to a quality or property that has the ability to do or affect something, or to act on a person or thing. Something that is powerful possesses might, vigor, and energy. It has force of character and produces an effect.[2] True preaching empowers and strengthens people savingly, spiritually, and practically. Calvin wrote, "Preaching is an instrument for effecting the salvation of the faithful, and though it can do nothing without the Spirit of God, yet through [the Spirit's] inward operation it produces the most powerful effects."[3] Calvin was distinguishing between the power of Spirit-anointed preaching and the power of man-centered preaching.

In his teaching about preaching, Calvin provided nine reasons why faithful, Spirit-anointed preaching is powerful. Let us consider these reasons.

---

1. *Inst.* 4.3.3.

2. J. A. Simpson and E. S. C. Weiner, *The Oxford English Dictionary,* 2nd ed. (Oxford: Clarendon Press, 1989), 12:259.

3. *Commentary* on Romans 11:14.

Reason #1: It Allows the Word of God to Set the Agenda

Sixteenth-century Geneva in the Swiss Alps was surrounded by a continent aflame with reformation. Roman Catholicism was weakening daily as men and women became Protestants. In many places, people's lives were endangered by this change of allegiance.

In Geneva, Calvin ascended a Protestant pulpit and preached several times a week. What was his preaching like? T. H. L. Parker ponders this question in the opening lines of his book *Calvin's Preaching*.[4]

What would we expect a Protestant to preach in the opening years of the Reformation? You might respond, "The gospel, of course!" But that betrays your familiarity with the beginning and the end of the Reformation story. Try for a minute to forget everything you know about the Reformation. Then imagine a movement in its infant stages that was rebelling against a massive religious establishment. The leaders of this movement communicated to their followers primarily through preaching. Wouldn't you expect that there would have been long discourses about the evils of the Roman Catholic Church, closely reasoned arguments for the superiority of Protestantism, maybe even a critique of the priest in the next village? But that is not what you would have found in Geneva during Calvin's time. Instead, in his preaching you would have found consecutive exposition of the Bible, week in and week out. Polemics were not excluded, to be sure, but they were not allowed to set the preaching agenda. The Word of God did that.

This was true even on the first Sunday that Calvin preached after returning to Geneva in 1541. What would Calvin say to a packed church? Would he rebuke Geneva's leaders for exiling him three years before? Would he chastise laypeople who had persistently mocked and rejected him? He did neither. Rather, Calvin simply picked up where he had left off three years earlier; he let the Word of God set the agenda. In doing so, he was true to his conviction, already stated in the first edition of his *Institutes of the Christian Religion*, that ministers' "whole task is limited to the ministry of God's Word; their whole

---

4. T. H. L. Parker, *Calvin's Preaching* (Louisville: Westminster/John Knox Press, 1992), 1.

wisdom to the knowledge of His Word; their whole eloquence, to its proclamation."[5]

Calvin wrote further, "A rule is prescribed to all God's servants that they bring not their own inventions, but simply deliver, as from hand to hand, what they have received from God."[6] The inevitable result of this rule is that preachers should be immersed in the Word and yearn to preach it frequently and faithfully, Calvin said. He lived out those convictions by preaching frequently himself. He preached from the New Testament on Sunday mornings, the Psalms on Sunday afternoons, and the Old Testament at 6 a.m. on five weekdays every other week. During his last stay in Geneva, from 1541 to 1564, Calvin preached about four thousand sermons, averaging nearly 170 a year. On his deathbed, he said his preaching was more significant than his writings.[7]

Calvin set up the entire Genevan system to emphasize preaching. The Genevan Ordinances stipulated that Sunday sermons be preached in each of the three churches at daybreak and again at 9 a.m. The children were catechized at noon; a third sermon was then preached in each church at 3 p.m. During the week, sermons were preached on Mondays, Wednesdays, and Fridays at varying hours so that they could be heard one after the other. People could take in three sermons in one day, if they desired. By the time Calvin died, at least one sermon was preached in every church in Geneva every day of the week.

Calvin also preached the Word faithfully, knowing that "as soon as men depart, even in the smallest degree from God's Word, they cannot preach anything but falsehoods, vanities, impostures, errors, and deceits."[8] He did not dare to depart from Scripture, both in his content and in his interpretation. On his deathbed, he said that, despite his faults (for which he requested forgiveness), he could truthfully confess that he had never knowingly falsified the interpretation of a single verse of Scripture throughout nearly thirty years of ministry.

---

5. John Calvin, *Institutes of the Christian Religion* (1536 ed.), trans. Ford Lewis Battles (Grand Rapids: Eerdmans, 1975), 195.

6. *Commentary* on Jeremiah 1:9–10.

7. William Bouwsma, *John Calvin: A Sixteenth-Century Portrait* (New York: Oxford University Press, 1988), 29.

8. *Commentary* on Jeremiah 14:14.

Since the Word of God set the agenda for preaching, Calvin preached in series from various Bible books, sometimes at considerable length. For example, he preached 353 sermons on Isaiah, 200 on Deuteronomy, 189 on Acts, 174 on Ezekiel, 159 on Job, 123 on Genesis, and 107 on 1 Samuel.[9] In the last fifteen years of his life, he also preached through Judges, 2 Samuel, 1 Kings, Psalms, Jeremiah, Lamentations, Daniel, Hosea, Joel, Amos, Obadiah, Jonah, Micah, Zephaniah, the Harmony of the Gospels, 1 and 2 Corinthians, Galatians, Ephesians, 1 and 2 Thessalonians, 1 and 2 Timothy, and Titus.[10] Throughout all of these series, Calvin clearly stated his major theme, then exegeted the meaning of a passage and explained how it applied to his listeners. Much like homilies in style, his sermons had no divisions or points other than what the text dictated. As Paul Fuhrmann writes, "They are properly homilies as in the ancient church: expositions of Bible passages [in] the light of grammar and history, [providing] application to the hearers' life situations."[11]

Calvin's sermons from 1549 to 1560 were carefully recorded by Denis de Raguenier and a group of his secretaries. His catalog of Calvin's sermons includes 2,042 entries, with 263 later additions. Nearly one thousand of these sermons have been lost. Most of the others have been printed, though a number of them have not yet been translated into English.[12]

Calvin's style of exposition, known as *lectio continua,* lacked major points and some cohesiveness because each message was not necessarily a self-contained unit. That kind of preaching might be a liability in

9. Robert L. Reymond, *John Calvin: His Life and Influence* (Ross-shire, Scotland: Christian Focus, 2004), 84.

10. Dawn DeVries, "Calvin's preaching," in *The Cambridge Companion to John Calvin*, ed. Donald C. McKim (Cambridge: Cambridge University Press, 2004), 111.

11. Paul T. Fuhrmann, "Calvin, Expositor of Scripture," *Interpretation* 6, 2 (Apr 1952):191.

12. For additional statistics on Calvin's sermons, see John H. Leith, "Calvin's Doctrine of the Proclamation of the Word and Its Significance for Today," in *John Calvin and the Church: A Prism of Reform* (Louisville: Westminster/John Knox, 1990), 206–207.

many pulpits today,[13] for Calvin's sermon structure was embedded in the text itself and seldom laid out before the people in clear points.[14] Nevertheless, his steady, verse-by-verse exposition had definite assets. It prevented him from skipping over difficult and controversial subjects, which ensured that the full counsel of God was heard.[15]

Because the Word of God set the agenda, Calvin was a careful exegete, a clear expositor, and a faithful applier of the Word. As the originator of grammatico-historical exegesis, he was exegetically accurate in ascertaining the major thought a biblical writer was conveying in a text in its context. He would then explain that thought clearly and objectively, using a literal hermeneutic and a limited number of cross-references within Scripture, salting all with reasonable deductions and persuasive reasoning.[16] Throughout, according to Steven J. Lawson, Calvin used familiar words, vivid expressions, provocative questions, simple restatements, limited quotations, an unspoken outline, seamless transitions, and focused intensity.[17] But Calvin didn't stop there. He crossed the bridge from the ancient audience to his contemporary congregation by applying the Word, using pastoral exhortation, personal examination, loving rebuke, and polemic confrontation. He concluded his sermons with succinct summations, pressing appeals, and climactic prayers.[18]

Letting the Word of God set the agenda allowed for a great deal of diversity in preaching. Listen to Calvin's loving, gentle admonition to pastors on how to preach within the confines of Scripture:

---

13. T. H. L. Parker says, "His sermons often lack unity of subject owing to two or three or more principal ideas appearing in the text" (*The Oracles of God: An Introduction to the Preaching of John Calvin* [London: Lutterworth Press, 1947], 71).

14. Harold Dekker, "Calvin's Sermons—Their Structure and Style," *The Calvin Forum* (May, 1951): 205.

15. Steven J. Lawson, *The Expository Genius of John Calvin* (Orlando, Fla.: Reformation Trust, 2007), 32.

16. Cf. ibid., 65–80.

17. Cf. ibid., 83–100.

18. Cf. ibid., 103–129.

> Let the pastors boldly dare all things by the Word of God, of which they are constituted administrators. Let them constrain all the power, glory, and excellence of the world to give place to and to obey the divine majesty of this Word. Let them enjoin everyone by it, from the highest to the lowest. Let them edify the body of Christ. Let them devastate Satan's reign. Let them pasture the sheep, kill the wolves, instruct and exhort the rebellious. Let them bind and loose, thunder and lightning, if necessary, but let them do all according to the Word of God.[19]

An average sermon of Calvin covered four or five verses in the Old Testament and two or three verses in the New Testament. His sermons, which were forty to sixty minutes long, were fairly short for his day (perhaps due to his asthmatic condition). He reportedly spoke "deliberately, often with long pauses to allow people to think," though others have said he must have spoken rapidly to complete his sermons on time.[20]

Calvin's style of preaching was plain and clear. In a sermon titled "Pure Preaching of the Word," Calvin wrote, "We must shun all unprofitable babbling, and stay ourselves upon plain teaching, which is forcible."[21] Rhetoric for its own sake or vain babbling must be avoided, though true eloquence, when subjected to the simplicity of the gospel, is to be coveted. When Joachim Westphal charged Calvin with "babbling" in his sermons, Calvin replied that he stuck to the main point of the text and practiced "cautious brevity."[22]

Calvin's sermons abounded with application. The application was usually direct and immediate. Phrases such as "So this [or that] is what we have to gather from this passage…" or "Let us learn from

19. Cited in Pierre Marcel, *The Relevance of Preaching* (New York: Westminster Publishing House, 2000), 59.

20. Philip Vollmer, *John Calvin: Theologian, Preacher, Educator Statesman* (Richmond: Presbyterian Committee of Publication, 1909), 124; George Johnson, "Calvinism and Preaching," *Evangelical Quarterly*, 4, 3 (July 1932): 249.

21. John Calvin, *The Mystery of Godliness* (Grand Rapids: Eerdmans, 1962), 55.

22. John C. Bowman, "Calvin as a Preacher," *Reformed Church Review* 56 (1909): 251–52.

this place…" were sprinkled throughout his sermons. In some messages, application took more time than exposition. Short, pungent applications constantly urged, exhorted, and invited sinners to act in obedience to God's Word. "We have not come to the preaching merely to hear what we do not know, but to be incited to do our duty," Calvin said to his flock.[23]

Parker suggests that Calvin's sermons followed a certain pattern:

1. Prayer.
2. Recapitulation of the previous sermon.
3a. Exegesis and exposition of the first point.
3b. Application of the first point and exhortation to obedience of duty.
4a. Exegesis and exposition of the second point.
4b. Application of the second point and exhortation to obedience of duty, etc.
5. Closing prayer, which contained a brief, implicit summary of the sermon.[24]

John Gerstner says that though Calvin often followed this structure, he frequently departed from it in preaching because "he was so eager to get at the application that he often introduced it in the midst of the exposition. In other words, application was the dominant element in the preaching of John Calvin to which all else was subordinated."[25]

Though Calvin faced much opposition after first returning to Geneva (1541–1555), his preaching was so powerful that most people in the city eventually were won over by it and allowed the Word of God to direct their lives. After 1555, Calvin worked steadily on promoting the Word of God in the pulpit, in the academy, in print, and in counseling. The result, James M. Boice writes, was that "under Calvin's preaching the city began to be transformed." As the people of Geneva learned God's Word and were changed by it, the city became,

---

23. *CO*, 79: 783.
24. Parker, *The Oracles of God*, 70–71.
25. John H. Gerstner, "Calvin's Two-Voice Theory of Preaching," *Reformed Review* 13, 2 (1959): 22.

as John Knox later said, "a New Jerusalem from which the gospel spread to the rest of Europe, England, and the New World."[26]

Reason #2: It Proclaims the Scriptures Authoritatively

The primary motivation of Calvin's preaching was theological; it was the conviction that, so long as preaching does not depart from Scripture, the preaching of the Word of God *is* the Word of God.[27] Calvin rooted this conviction in the Old Testament prophets. God did not normally speak in Old Testament times through thunder but through His prophets, he said. As a true prophet spoke God's Word, God so intimately identified with what the prophet spoke that the prophet's mouth became God's mouth. As Calvin said in his commentary on Isaiah, "The Word goeth out of the mouth of God in such a manner that it likewise goeth out of the mouth of men; for God does not speak openly from heaven but employs men as his instruments."[28] In commenting on the power of Haggai's words to arouse people to build the temple, Calvin said, "The Word of God is not distinguished from the word of the prophet."[29] He explained: "The message of the prophet obtained as much power as though God descended from heaven, and had given manifest tokens of His presence. We may then conclude from these words, that the glory of God so shines in His Word, that we ought to be so much affected by it, whenever He speaks by His servants, as though He were nigh to us, face to face."[30]

In the New Testament era, God's Word also is proclaimed by messengers, especially preachers of the gospel. Calvin commented: "When the prophet says *by the breath of His lips,* this must not be limited to the person of Christ; for it refers to the Word which is preached by His ministers. Christ acts by them in such a manner that

26. James M. Boice, *Whatever Happened to the Gospel of Grace? Rediscovering the Doctrines that Shook the World* (Wheaton, Ill.: Crossway Books, 2001), 83–84.

27. Cf. Leroy Nixon, *John Calvin, Expository Preacher* (Grand Rapids: Eerdmans, 1950), 49–51.

28. *Commentary* on Isaiah 55:11.

29. *Commentary* on Haggai 1:12.

30. Ibid.

He wishes their *mouth* to be reckoned as His *mouth,* and their *lips* as His *lips.*"[31]

Why did God choose to use sinful men to be preachers of His Word? Calvin provides three reasons, which are summarized well by Dawn DeVries:

> First, in this way he [God] provides for our weakness in that he prefers "to address us in human fashion through interpreters in order to draw us to himself, rather than to thunder at us and drive us away."[32] Second, God uses human ministers to exercise our humility, [for] "when a puny man risen from the dust speaks in God's name, at this point we best evidence our piety and obedience toward God if we show ourselves teachable toward his minister, although he excels us in nothing."[33] Finally, the human ministry serves as a bond of union between believers, knitting the church together into a cohesive community. If each person were able to interpret the written Scripture for himself, each would go off on his own and despise the others. Instead, God joins all believers together to one who is appointed pastor to teach the rest, and the benefits of salvation are communicated to the many through the service of the one. The ministry of the Word, then, is like a sinew that holds tissue and bones together in one body.[34]

Preaching is the Word of God for two important reasons, Calvin said. First, preaching is the Word of God because the content of preaching is the exposition and interpretation of the Word of God. That exposition and interpretation is never to be regarded as new revelation but simply as an explanation of what God reveals in His Word.[35] The

---

31. *Commentary* on Isaiah 11:4.

32. *Institutes of the Christian Religion* [hereafter *Inst.*], ed. John T. McNeill and trans. Ford Lewis Battles (Philadelphia: Westminster Press, 1960), Book 4, chapter 1, section 5. Hereafter the format *Inst.* 4.1.5 will be used.

33. *Inst.* 4.3.1.

34. *Inst.* 4.3.2; DeVries, "Calvin's preaching," 108.

35. *Commentary* on John 16:12; cf. Benjamin Charles Milner, Jr., *Calvin's Doctrine of the Church* (Leiden: Brill, 1970), 102–103; Kenneth Alan Kok, "*Praedicatio Verbi Dei:* The Nature and Authority of Preaching in Calvin's Theology" (Th.M. thesis, Westminster Theological Seminary, 1985), 75.

canon of Scripture has long been closed; the age of special revelation was complete after John wrote Revelation. Hence, the preached Word does not rival the written Word but derives its authority from it. It is thus called the Word of God "derivatively or by association."[36] That authority is absolute, since, due to the testimony of the Spirit, Scripture calls for complete credence and total submission.[37] In Parker's words, preaching has no authority in itself, but rather "borrows" its authority from the written Word and thus is the Word of God when it remains faithful to God's revelation.[38] Sound preaching, therefore, is *God speaking* in the way He now normally speaks to us. Having resigned His office of speaking directly to preachers,[39] "God does not wish to be heard but by the voice of His ministers," Calvin said.[40]

Calvin thus regarded the preaching of Scripture as living speech from one person to others.[41] He wrote, "We preach as if God were here present; as if a secretary were speaking before a prince;... as if we were an organ of He who has sovereign authority."[42]

Second, preaching is the Word of God because the preacher is called, appointed, and sent by God to do this task. The preacher is ordained as the herald of Christ and thus has the authority and responsibility to speak in Christ's name. This high view of the ministry means that a true preacher is a specially commissioned ambassador of God (an image Calvin liked to use) to be the mouthpiece of God to His people. Ronald Wallace thus says: "The task of the preacher of the Word is to expound the Scripture in the midst of the worshiping Church, preaching in the expectancy that God will do, through his frail human word, what He did through the Word of His prophets of old, that God by His grace will cause the word that goes out of

36. Parker, *The Oracles of God,* 50.

37. T. H. L. Parker, *Calvin's Preaching* (Louisville: Westminster John Knox, 1992), 2–5.

38. Ibid., 23, 40–41.

39. *Commentary* on Acts 13:47.

40. *Commentary* on Genesis 9:12; Isaiah 50:10.

41. George Johnson, "Calvinism and Preaching," *Evangelical Quarterly* 4, 3 (1932): 250.

42. Cited in ibid.; *CR,* 79:783.

the mouth of man to become also a Word that proceeds from God Himself, with all the power and efficacy of the Word of the Creator and Redeemer."[43]

Preaching is imbued with an incredible, overwhelming, even terrifying authority. None of this authority comes from the preacher, however, but from the Word. Servants of the Word therefore ought to humble themselves before the prospect of handling that Word, in view of their awesome task. Parker writes: "For Calvin the message of Scripture is sovereign over the congregation and sovereign over the preacher. His humility is shown by his submitting to this authority."[44]

Calvin was a prime example of this humility. As Lawson writes: "The understanding of the preacher's role produced a profound sense of humility in Calvin as he rose to preach. He saw himself as standing *under* the authority of the Word."[45]

Because of its authority, the Word of God must never be handled lightly or irreverently. The following quote from Calvin clearly demonstrates his convictions and is a sobering message for today's preachers:

> Neither sun or moon, light though they give to the earth, so show God's majesty as do the Law, the Prophets, and the Gospel. And yet how will people speak of it? With what audacity? I ask you, do not men today give themselves license to speak of God's name at their own fancy? And when they start arguing about Holy Scripture over a glass of wine in a tavern or at their tables, is there any question of humbling themselves and of knowing their ignorance and their infirmity and begging God to give his Holy Spirit so that his secrets may be dealt with by us as they should be? No; those arguments are mere mockery.[46]

---

43. Ronald S. Wallace, *Calvin's Doctrine of the Word and Sacrament* (Edinburgh: Oliver and Boyd, 1953), 83.

44. Parker, *Calvin's Preaching*, 39; cf. 44.

45. Lawson, *The Expository Genius of John Calvin,* 26 (emphasis in original).

46. John Calvin, "Sermon XXXIII; on the Third Commandment, Deut. 5.11," in *Ioannis Calvini opera quae supersunt omnia*, ed. Wilhelm Baum, Edward Cunitz, and Edward Reuss, *Corpus Reformatorum*, vols. 29–87 (Brunsvigae:

Calvin believed that proclaiming the Word of God demands three critical prerequisites: great reverence, soul preparation, and hard work. "In Calvin's view, to explore the height, depth, width, and breadth of the Bible was to revere its supernatural Author," Lawson writes.[47] For soul preparation, Calvin maintained that a preacher should "speak not so much with the mouth, as with the dispositions of the heart." He was well aware that a sermon seldom rises higher than the condition, communion, and devotion of a preacher's soul before God.[48] And the image of the preacher as a pastor and teacher moved Calvin to emphasize careful sermon preparation as a sacred and diligent responsibility. "The office of teaching is committed to pastors for no other purpose than that God alone may be heard there," Calvin said.[49]

Calvin had a heavy preaching schedule and a difficult workload, but he obviously studied every text he expounded with great care and widely read what others had said about it. He once said, "If I should enter the pulpit without deigning to look at a book and should frivolously think to myself, 'Oh, well, when I preach, God will give me enough to say,' and come here without troubling to read or think what I ought to declare, and do not carefully consider how I must apply Holy Scripture to the edification of the people, then I should be an arrogant upstart."[50]

Calvin preached extemporaneously, relying heavily on his remarkable memory. He often declared that the power of God could best be exhibited in extemporaneous delivery, but that was never an excuse for sloppy preparation. "No one will ever be a good minister of the Word except he first be a scholar," Calvin said. The pastor "ought to be prepared by long study for giving to the people, as out of a storehouse, a variety of instruction concerning the Word of God."[51]

C.A. Schwetschke and Son, 1863–1900), 26.281–82 (hereafter *CO*); cited in Parker, 38.

47. Lawson, *The Expository Genius of John Calvin*, 27.

48. Ibid., 40.

49. *Inst.* 4.1.9.

50. Quoted in Parker, *Calvin's Preaching*, 81.

51. J. Graham Miller, *Calvin's Wisdom: An Anthology Arranged Alphabetically* (Edinburgh: Banner of Truth, 1992), 256.

In a recent address, R. Albert Mohler Jr. noted that Calvin never apologized for the importance of study and learning: "The right kind of learning is necessary for one to be able to rightly divide the Word of truth, rightly to preach, to know the difference between true and false piety and true and false doctrine. Calvin said that to be a minister of the divine Word, the one who would preach must be a student of the Scriptures, one who has not only a passing knowledge of these things but a confident knowledge, and rises to the pulpit as one who has authority—indeed, not the authority of his learning but of the Word of God and of his calling, demonstrated in the fact that he knows of which he speaks."[52]

Though most church attenders can glean much from the Word of God, the ministry of the Word is still a great gift to the church, Calvin said, because studious, Spirit-anointed ministers who instruct their congregations as Philip did the eunuch or as fathers do their children can shed a great deal more light on the Scriptures. Calvin reasoned: "Since we ought to be satisfied with the Word of God alone, what purpose is served by hearing sermons every day, or even the office of pastors? Has not every person the opportunity of reading the Bible? But Paul assigns to teachers the duty of dividing or cutting, as if a father in giving food to his children were dividing the bread and cutting it in small pieces."[53]

If the minister works hard to bring his congregation, by the authority of God, the very Word of God, he should expect fruit from his preaching, for Christ will honor it and bless it, Calvin said. Though Christ goes forth to sow as in the parable of Matthew 13, ministers are also sowers of the Word. Consequently, Christ "makes use of our exertions and employs us as His instruments for cultivating His field, so that He alone acts by us and in us."[54] When the faithful minister of Christ preaches the Word of Christ, "the word of the preacher should be heard, in the expectancy that Christ the Mediator will come and

52. Ligonier's National Conference Address, March 19, 2009.

53. *Commentary* on 2 Timothy 2:15.

54. *Commentary* on Matthew 13:37.

give His presence where the gospel is preached, and cause men to hear His voice through the voice of the minister."[55]

Reason #3: It Co-labors with the Holy Spirit

A person must be qualified to be God's mouthpiece. He must be converted and "endowed with the Spirit,"[56] which necessitates being called to the ministry and having "the interior power of the Spirit conjoined with his external voice," so that he becomes "the instrument of God."[57]

Calvin repeatedly stressed that preaching can be effectual only when the Holy Spirit, who is Christ's heaven-sent minister, sovereignly and graciously blesses it. Thus, two ministers are appointed by God to preach each sermon. The Holy Spirit is the "internal minister" who uses the "external minister" to preach God's Word, Calvin said. The external minister "holds forth the vocal word and it is received by the ears," but the internal minister "truly communicates the thing proclaimed [which] is Christ."[58]

So God speaks through the mouth of His servants by His Word and Spirit. "Wherever the gospel is preached, it is as if God himself came into the midst of us," Calvin wrote.[59] Preaching is the instrument and the authority that the Spirit uses in His saving work of illuminating, converting, and sealing sinners. "There is...an inward efficacy of the Holy Spirit when he sheds forth his power upon hearers, that they may embrace a discourse [sermon] by faith."[60]

Calvin said the preached Word and the inner testimony of the Spirit may be distinguished from one another, but they cannot be separated. Word and Spirit are organically joined; without the Spirit, the preached Word only adds to the condemnation of unbelievers. On

55. Wallace, *Calvin's Doctrine of the Word and Sacrament*, 83.

56. *Commentary* on Luke 24:49.

57. *Commentary* on Psalm 105:31.

58. John Calvin, *Tracts and Treatises*, trans. Henry Beveridge (Grand Rapids: Eerdmans, 1958), 1:173.

59. *Commentary on Synoptic Gospels*, 3:129.

60. *Commentary* on Ezekiel 1:3.

the other hand, Calvin admonished radicals who accented the Spirit at the expense of the Word, saying that only the spirit of Satan separates itself from the Word.[61]

For much of his life, Calvin opposed three groups in Europe who did not maintain this biblical balance between Word and Spirit.[62] First, he opposed enthusiasts who believed that the Spirit would speak directly to each individual believer, thus negating the need for special preachers. Though Calvin appreciated their recognition of the need for the Holy Spirit, he thoroughly disagreed with their dismissal of the preaching office.

Second, Calvin disagreed with those who argued that Christians should simply read the Bible on their own and do away with preachers and teachers. Calvin said preachers and teachers are God's gift to the church and are specially commissioned by God to teach His Word and exhort His people from it.

Third, Calvin disagreed with the Roman Catholic Church, which taught that congregations should unquestioningly accept everything taught by the clergy since they were supposedly guided by the Spirit. Though Calvin had a high view of preaching, he was not ignorant of the possibility that preachers might err in their expositions. Thus, he encouraged his congregations to examine what they heard from their preachers in the light of God's written Word.

Reason #4: It Guarantees the Church's Fruitfulness

For Calvin, the preached Word is powerful to effect what God promises or commands. God's preached Word and His actions in the church are inseparable. Preaching is at the heart of the church's fruitfulness in at least three ways:

- Preaching is the heart of worship. Calvin believed the central focus of the Reformation was the renewal of worship. Worship is central to our purpose on earth, and preaching

61. Kok, "The Nature and Authority of Preaching," 79; Willem Balke, "Het Pietisme in Oostfriesland," *Theologia Reformata* 21 (1978): 320–27.

62. Cf. Randall Zachman, *John Calvin as Teacher, Pastor, and Theologian* (Grand Rapids: Baker Academic, 2006).

is central for worship, he said. Without it, worship would lack its ordinance to convert and nurture people. "There is nothing more notable or glorious in the church than the ministry of the gospel," Calvin concluded.[63]

For Calvin, worship involves more than restoring the pulpit to the center of the sanctuary. Preaching time in the worship service must be jealously guarded. No other element of worship should be allowed to impinge on this sacred time.

- Preaching converts sinners. The Holy Spirit uses preaching to plant saving faith. Under the Spirit's tutelage, preaching leads to the regeneration of sinners. God uses preaching to create and gather His church. So Calvin wrote, "We cannot be Christians without regeneration, for the Gospel is not preached only in order to be heard by us, but that it may radically reform our hearts as a seed of immortal life."[64]

  Through preaching, the Holy Spirit established the church wherever Jesus and His apostles went to proclaim the Word. That is still going on today through ministers. Calvin wrote, "Christ through our instrumentality, illuminates the minds of men, renews their hearts, and in short regenerates them wholly."[65] How powerful the preached Word is in converting the human soul!

- Preaching edifies saints. Parker says Calvin loved to focus on the edification of saints, but he put more into it than is often understood today. For Calvin, edification meant building up or constructing the church in faith and holiness (oikodomeo) so that the Word would be profitable. God is the primary actor in edification; He uses the preacher only as a tool to strengthen saving faith and to promote sanctification.[66]

  Through preaching, God establishes His throne in the hearts and lives of His own. "Christ does not otherwise rule among us than by the doctrine of the Gospel," Calvin

63. *Inst.* 4.3.3.
64. *Commentary* on 1 Peter 1:23.
65. *Commentary* on 2 Corinthians 3:6.
66. Parker, *Calvin's Preaching*, 46–47.

wrote.[67] Preaching is God's grand ordinance that He uses to uphold, rule, nurture, defend, assure, and preserve His church. So Calvin said, "As often then as God's fatherly love towards us is preached, let us know that there is given to us ground for true joy, that with peaceable consciences we may be certain of our salvation."[68] Saints are strengthened in faith and mature through the powerful proclamation of God's Word. As Calvin wrote, "Christ reigns whenever He subdues the world to Himself by the preaching of the gospel."[69]

Reason #5: It Impacts the Nations

Preaching has international results. Wallace says Calvin taught that preaching "in a hidden way directs the whole course of history and creates the disturbance amongst the nations that is to bring about the consummation of His eternal purpose. Preaching is the *banner which shall stand for an ensign to the peoples....* [It is] also the sword in the hand of the Church by which secretly and unknown even to itself the Church rules or brings judgment amongst the nations."[70]

God uses the sword of preaching on His fallen creation by saving and destroying nations. Calvin said, "He shall smite the wicked with the Word of His mouth and shall slay them with the breath of His lips."[71] But he added, "Heaven and earth are said to be restored by the doctrine of salvation; because in Christ, as Paul says, are collected all things that are either in heaven or earth.... Since, therefore, the whole face of the world is disfigured, there are good grounds for saying that godly teachers renovate the world.... Thus, the heavens are said to be planted and the earth to be founded when the Lord establishes the Church by the Word."[72]

Powerful preaching therefore has a twofold effect. No one hears the preached Word without effect, for the Word either saves or condemns,

67. *Commentary* on Micah 4:3.
68. *Commentary* on John 15:21.
69. *Commentary* on Acts 1:8.
70. Wallace, *Calvin's Doctrine of the Word and Sacrament*, 86.
71. *Commentary* on Isaiah 11:4.
72. *Commentary* on Isaiah 51:16.

renews or hardens. The preached Word is either a savor of life to life or a savor of death to death.[73] Preaching's validity, therefore, does not depend on how people respond to it. Preaching makes the godly more godly and makes the ungodly more ungodly. Calvin wrote, "As the Word is efficacious for the salvation of believers, so it is abundantly efficacious for the condemning of the wicked."[74]

Nothing is worse than rejecting the preached Word, Calvin said. Through rejection, the world is constantly ripening for judgment. Since the Word is the scepter of Christ's kingdom, "it cannot be rejected without treating Him with open contempt," Calvin said, for "No crime is more offensive to God than contempt of His Word."[75]

The preached Word is also powerful to the reprobate, as well as frightening and agonizing. In commenting on Hebrews 4:12, Calvin offered this graphic picture of the reprobate under the Word:

> The reprobate...though not softened, set up a brazen and an iron heart against God's Word, [yet are] restrained by their own guilt. They indeed laugh but it is a sardonic laugh; for they inwardly feel that they are, as it were, slain; they make evasions in various ways so as not to come before God's tribunal; but though unwilling they are yet dragged there by this very Word which they arrogantly deride; so that they may be fitly compared to furious dogs, which bite and claw the chain by which they are bound and yet can do nothing—they still remain fast bound.[76]

Reason #6: It Moves People to Truly Hear God's Word

For Calvin, Parker says, "the preacher is only half of the Church's activity of proclamation. He has received God's message from Holy Scripture and is now handing it on to others. These others, the members of the congregation, form the other half."[77]

Calvin often preached to his congregation about their responsibility to hear the Word of God aright. He taught his members in what spirit

73. *Commentary* on 2 Corinthians 2:15.
74. *Commentary* on Isaiah 55:11.
75. *Commentary* on Matthew 10:14.
76. *Commentary* on Hebrews 4:12.
77. Parker, *Calvin's Preaching*, 48.

they should come to the sermon, what to listen for in preaching, and what was expected of those who hear. Since true preaching is biblical preaching and ministers are to preach only what God commands by opening His Word, people must test sermons by this criterion, Calvin said. They must reject unscriptural sermons and accept and obey scriptural sermons. Calvin's goal was that the people would grasp the importance of preaching, desire it as a supreme blessing, and participate as actively in the sermon as the preacher himself. Since listening is an act of faith, they should have the "willingness to obey God completely and with no reserve," Calvin said.[78] Church members must be good pupils who sit at the feet of the preacher as if at the feet of Jesus Christ, their "sovereign Teacher," for their own edification and the glory of the triune God. In short, a church member should have the same purpose while listening to the preacher as the minister has while preaching. The minister and the people should not be at cross-purposes with each other.[79]

Faith, obedience, and good works are the fruit of Spirit-empowered listening. Benjamin Milner summarizes Calvin, saying, "Preaching is the 'mother' of faith,[80] and has for its 'goal' 'that believers should exercise themselves in good works.'"[81]

Though the preacher should tell people how to listen, many of those who listen will not live up to what they hear. Calvin stressed the importance of profitable hearing of the Word because he knew few people hear well. Calvin said, "If the same sermon is preached, say, to a hundred people, twenty receive it with the ready obedience of faith, while the rest hold it valueless, or laugh, or hiss, or loathe it."[82] More than forty such comments appear in Calvin's sermons (especially on Deuteronomy), commentaries (e.g., on Ps. 119:101 and Acts 11:23), and the *Institutes* (especially 3.21 to 3.24). If profitable hearing was a problem in Calvin's day, how much more is it so today, when a

78. Leroy Nixon, *John Calvin: Expository Preacher* (Grand Rapids: Eerdmans, 1950), 65.

79. Parker, *Calvin's Preaching*, 50–53.

80. *Commentary* on 2 Corinthians 13:5.

81. *Commentary* on Titus 3:8; Milner, *Calvin's Doctrine of the Church*, 106.

82. *Inst.* 3.24.12.

minister must compete for a congregation's attention in the midst of the mass media that bombard us on a daily basis! How desperately both preachers and hearers need to pray for the Holy Spirit to help them worship in accord with God's purposes.

Reason #7: It is Experiential

Experiential or experimental preaching addresses how a Christian experiences the truth of Christian doctrine in his life. The term *experimental* comes from the Latin *experimentum*, meaning "trial." It is derived from the verb *experior*, meaning "to try, prove, or put to the test." The same verb also can mean "to find or know by experience," thus leading to the word *experientia*, meaning "knowledge gained by experiment." Calvin used *experiential* and *experimental* interchangeably, since both words indicate the need for measuring experienced knowledge against the touchstone of Scripture.

Experimental preaching stresses the need to know the great truths of the Word of God by experience. It seeks to explain in terms of biblical truth how spiritual matters ought to go, how they do go, and the goal of the Christian life. It aims to apply divine truth to the entire range of the believer's personal experience, as well as to his relationships with family, the church, and the world around him.

Experiential preaching is discriminatory

For Calvin, experiential preaching does two things. First, it *discriminates* between the believer and the unbeliever. That is, it clearly defines the difference between a Christian and non-Christian, opening the kingdom of heaven to one and shutting it to the other. Discriminatory preaching offers forgiveness of sins and eternal life to all who embrace Christ as Savior and Lord by true faith, but it also proclaims the wrath of God and His eternal condemnation on those who are unbelieving, unrepentant, and unconverted. Such preaching teaches that unless our religion is experiential, we will perish—not because experience itself saves, but because the Christ who saves sinners must be personally experienced as the foundation on which the house of our eternal hope is built (Matt. 7:22–27; 1 Cor. 1:30; 2:2).

The genuineness of faith is not easily dissected and understood, Calvin admitted. The experience of faith contains numerous paradoxes that powerful preaching does not hesitate to address. For example, a paradox exists in the life of faith when we are called to believe that God is still with us when we feel that He has deserted us. Another paradox exists when we believe that God is favorably inclined to us and then He strips us of all consciousness of that favor and seems to postpone fulfilling His merciful promises.[83]

The believer can experience such paradoxes on a daily basis, Calvin said. He can feel forsaken of God, even when he knows deep within that he is not (Isa. 49:14–16). Conflicting experiences, such as hope and fear, seem to cancel each other out. If fear gets the upper hand, Calvin said, we should throw ourselves wholly on the promises of God.[84] Those promises will give us courage to go on in spite of the temptation to doubt. Moreover, it is when we acknowledge God by faith, though we cannot see or feel His goodness and power, that we truly honor His lordship and His Word.[85] To believe in God when experience seems to annul His promises takes great faith, but this experience of faith is precisely what enables believers to remain undisturbed when their entire world is shaken.[86]

Calvin was acutely aware that a person may think that the Father has entrusted him to Christ when such is not the case. It is one thing to stress Christ's task in salvation and quite another to know whether a person has been joined to Christ by true faith. Many people appear to be in Christ when they are really estranged from Him. Calvin said, "It daily happens that those who seemed to be Christ's fall away from him again.... Such persons never cleaved to Christ with the heartfelt trust in which certainty of salvation has, I say, been established for us."[87]

For Calvin, what appears to be faith often lacks a saving character. He thus spoke of faith that is unformed, implicit, temporary, illusion-

83. *CO*, 31:344.
84. *CO*, 31:548.
85. *CO*, 31:525.
86. *CO*, 31:703; 32:194.
87. *Inst.* 3.24.7.

ary, false, shadowy, transitory, and under a cloak of hypocrisy.[88] Self-deception is a distinct possibility, Calvin said. Because the reprobate often feel something like the faith of the elect,[89] self-examination is essential. So Calvin wrote, "Let us learn to examine ourselves, and to search whether those interior marks by which God distinguishes his children from strangers belong to us, viz., the living root of piety and faith."[90] Happily, the truly saved are delivered from self-deception through proper examination directed by the preacher and the Holy Spirit. Calvin said, "In the meantime, the faithful are taught to examine themselves with solicitude and humility, lest carnal security insinuate itself, instead of the assurance of faith."[91]

Even when directing self-examination, Calvin said, the preacher must emphasize Christ. We must examine ourselves to see whether we are placing our trust in *Christ alone*, for this is the fruit of biblical experience. Anthony Lane says that for Calvin, self-examination is not so much "Am I *trusting* in Christ?" as it is "Am I trusting in *Christ*?"[92] Self-examination must always direct us to Christ and His promises. It must not be done apart from the help of the Holy Spirit, who alone can shed light on Christ's saving work in a believer's soul. Apart from Christ, the Word, and the Spirit, Calvin said, "if you contemplate yourself, that is sure damnation."[93]

---

88. *Inst.* 3.2.3, 5, 10–11. For Calvin on temporary faith, see David Foxgrover, "'Temporary Faith' and the Certainty of Salvation," *Calvin Theological Journal* 15 (1980): 220–32; A. N. S. Lane, "Calvin's Doctrine of Assurance," *Vox Evangelica* 11 (1979): 45–46; K. Exalto, *De Zekerheid des Geloofs bij Calvijn* (Apeldoorn, The Netherlands: Willem de Zwijgerstichting, 1978), 15–20, 27–30.

89. *Inst.* 3.2.11.

90. *Commentary* on Ezekiel 13:9. David Foxgrover shows that Calvin relates the need for self-examination to a great variety of topics: knowledge of God and ourselves, judgment, repentance, confession, affliction, the Lord's Supper, providence, duty, the kingdom of God, etc. ("John Calvin's Understanding of Conscience" [Ph.D. dissertation, Claremont, 1978], 312ff.). Cf. J. P. Pelkonen, "The Teaching of John Calvin on the Nature and Function of the Conscience," *Lutheran Quarterly* 21 (1969): 24–88.

91. *Inst.* 3.2.7.

92. Lane, "Calvin's Doctrine of Assurance," 47.

93. *Inst.* 3.2.24.

Experiential preaching is applicatory

Second, experiential preaching *applies* the Word. It applies the text to every aspect of a listener's life, promoting a religion that is a power and not mere form (2 Tim. 3:5). Robert Burns defined such religion as "Christianity brought home to men's business and bosoms," and said the principle on which it rests is "that Christianity should not only be known, and understood, and believed, but also felt, and enjoyed, and practically applied."[94]

Experiential preaching, then, says the Christian faith must be experienced, tasted, and lived through the saving power of the Holy Spirit. It stresses scriptural truth, "which is able to make us wise unto salvation through faith in Christ Jesus" (2 Tim. 3:15). Preaching teaches us that Christ, who is the living Word (John 1:1) and the very embodiment of the truth, must be experientially known and embraced. It proclaims the need for sinners to experience who God is in His Son. As John 17:3 says, "This is life eternal, that they might know thee the only true God, and Jesus Christ, whom thou hast sent." The word *know* in this text, as well as in other biblical passages, does not indicate a casual acquaintance, but an intimate, personal knowledge of God in Christ.

Such knowledge is never divorced from Scripture. According to Isaiah 8:20, all of our beliefs, including our experiences, must be tested against Holy Scripture. That is what the word *experimental* intends to convey. Just as scientific experimentation tests a hypothesis against a body of evidence, so experimental preaching involves examining Christian experience in light of the teaching of the Word of God.

Calvin valued experience so long as it is rooted in Scripture and springs out of the living reality of faith. He repeatedly defined the experience of believers as something beyond verbal expression. For example, he wrote: "Such, then, is a conviction that requires no reasons, such a knowledge with which the best reason agrees—in which the mind truly reposes, more securely and constantly than in any reasons: such finally, a feeling that can be born only of heavenly revelation. I speak of nothing other than what each believer experiences

94. Robert Burns, "Introduction," in *The Works of Thomas Halyburton* (London: Thomas Tegg, 1835), xiv–xv.

within himself—though my words fall far beneath a just explanation of the matter."[95] Calvin went on to say that a believer's recognition of God "consists more in living experience than in vain and high-flown speculations." But he hastened to add, "Indeed, with experience as our teacher, we find God just as he declares himself in his Word."[96]

Unbiblical experience fabricates a god that does not square with the Scriptures, but true experience always flows out of the truths of Scripture and underscores them. Holy Scripture is consistent with sacred Spirit-worked experience, since the Bible is not a book of abstract or scholastic doctrines but a book of doctrines that is rooted in real, experiential daily living. Thus, experience played an important role in Calvin's exegesis. Willem Balke writes: "Experience can serve as a hermeneutical key in the explanation of the Scriptures. The Bible places us in the center of the struggle of faith, *coram Deo*, and therefore Calvin can recommend himself as exegete as he does in the introduction to the Commentary on the Psalms (1557) since he has experienced what the Bible testifies."[97]

Calvin viewed his experiences as a Reformer as an important qualification for preaching God's Word. Though he related his experiential qualification particularly to the Psalms, since the Psalms relate best to the suffering people of God and are, as he calls them, "an anatomy of all parts of the soul,"[98] all of his sermons and commentaries reveal that he believed no book of Scripture could be reduced to mere doctrine.

Though Calvin valued experience in his exegesis and preaching, he understood that experience had limitations. When divorced from the Word, experience is altogether unreliable and is always incomplete. Calvin concluded that the depths of the human heart—always a focal point for the mystic—are not the way to God. Rather, he agreed with

95. *Inst.* 1.7.5.

96. *Inst.* 1.10.2.

97. Willem Balke, "The Word of God and *Experientia* according to Calvin," in *Calvinus Ecclesiae Doctor*, ed. W. H. Neuser (Kampen: Kok, 1978), 22. Much of what I write in this subheading is a summary of Balke's helpful effort to grapple with Calvin's understanding of experience in the life of the believer.

98. *Commentary* on Psalms, vol. 1, intro.

Martin Luther that the only way to God is Word-centered faith. The believer does not learn God's will from "*nuda experientia,*" Calvin said, but only through the testimony of Scripture.[99]

If Scripture is not the foundation of our experience of faith, we will be left with vague feelings that have no anchor, Calvin said. True faith anchors itself in the Word. We should not measure the presence of God in our lives by our experience, for that would soon bring us to despair. "If we should measure out the help of God according to our feelings," Calvin wrote, "our faith would soon waver and we would have no courage or hope."[100] He was careful not to call attention to his own experiences. Calvin avoided both experientialism and dry scholasticism. He did not see the Bible as a collection of doctrines but viewed biblical doctrines as "embedded in the life and faith of the church and of the individual, in the natural habitat of the verification of faith in Christian and ecclesiastical existence."[101]

The experience or sense of faith (*experientia fide* or *sensus fide*), according to Calvin, is inseparable from the ministry of the Holy Spirit. The Spirit renews the very core of man. That work involves the Spirit's illumination of the mind and His efficacious work in the heart. The Spirit's sealing work certifies the authority of the Word and the reality of the Spirit's saving work. It promotes confidence in God's promises of mercy and experiences of them. This doctrine, Calvin said, is "not of the tongue, but of life. It is not apprehended by the understanding and memory alone, as other disciplines are, but it is received only when it possesses the whole soul, and finds a seat and resting place in the inmost affection of the heart."[102]

Experientia fide is thus not due to a believer's own ability, but is the creative effect of the Spirit who uses the Word. It contains both objective and subjective truth. The Spirit testifies to the Word of God and to the heart of the believer, and the believer hears and experiences its reality. Through the Spirit's objective and subjective testimony, the

99. *CO*, 31:424.

100. *CO*, 31:103.

101. Balke, "The Word of God and *Experientia* according to Calvin," 22.

102. *Inst.* 3.6.4.

believer is experientially persuaded of the absolute truth of God and of His Word. Made willing by the powerful operations of the Spirit, the heart, will, and emotions respond in faith and obedience to the triune God. The Spirit is the Spirit of the Son, and His great task is to lead the believer to Christ, and through Him to the Father. Therefore, the center of faith's experience is having "fellowship with the Father and the Son" (1 John 1:3). True experience leads, then, to true communion and the practice of piety (*praxis pietatis*).

Reason #8: It Promotes Piety

True religion is fellowship between God and man. Fellowship that moves from God to man is *revelation*, Calvin said, whereas fellowship that moves from man to God, which involves man's obedient response, is *piety*. This piety functions by faith through God's grace and involves such devout acts as childlike trust, humble adoration, godly fear, and undying love. Calvin's applications in preaching aimed at exciting those kinds of graces.

Calvin said the goal of the preacher is to promote such piety, while remaining acutely aware that a listener cannot produce this piety himself. He is only a recipient of such piety by the grace of the Holy Spirit. Nevertheless, the Spirit accompanies the Word with the divine gift of pious graces.

Calvin's piety, like his theology, is inseparable from the knowledge of God. True knowledge of God results in pious activity that stretches beyond personal salvation to embrace the glory of God. Where God's glory is not served, piety cannot exist. Piety compels discipline, obedience, and love in every sphere of the believer's life. For Calvin, the law gives love the mandate and content to act, to obey God out of discipline, and so to live to His glory. Indeed, love is the fulfillment of the law. Thus, for Calvin, true piety is both vertical (Godward) and horizontal (manward); it is a relationship of love and law.

Grace and law, therefore, were both prominent in Calvin's theology and preaching. Keeping the law is especially important, he believed, because it leads us to consecrate our entire lives to God. Lionel Greve writes, "Grace has priority in such a way that Calvin's piety may be considered as a quality of life and response to God's grace that transcended law but at the same time included it." Greve continues: "Calvin's piety may be termed 'transcendent piety.' It transcends the creature because it is founded in grace but yet includes the creature as he is the subject of faithfulness. He is the subject in such a way that his piety is never primarily for his welfare.... The general movement of Calvin's piety is always God-ward. The benefits of God's goodness are merely byproducts of the main purpose—glorifying God."[103]

It is no wonder, then, that Calvin often opened his lectures on the Word with this prayer: "Grant us, Lord, to meditate on the heavenly mysteries of Thy wisdom, with true progress in piety, to Thy glory and our edification. Amen."[104]

Reason #9: It Aims for God's Glory

In all his sermons, Calvin kept three goals in mind: to glorify God, to edify believers by helping them grow in faith and in holiness, and to unite sinners with Christ so "that men be reconciled to God by the free remission of sins."[105] This aim of saving sinners, edifying saints, and glorifying the Trinity blended with Calvin's emphasis on scriptural doctrines. He said ministers are "keepers of the truth of God; that is to say, of his precious image, of that which concerneth the majesty of the doctrine of our salvation, and the life of the world."[106] Calvin frequently admonished them to keep this treasure safe by handling the Word of God carefully, always striving for pure, biblical teaching. That did not exclude preaching on contemporary events, however. As current events related to the passage being expounded, Calvin felt

103. Lionel Greve, "Freedom and Discipline in the Theology of John Calvin, William Perkins, and John Wesley: An Examination of the Origin and Nature of Pietism" (Ph.D. dissertation, Hartford Seminary Foundation, 1976), 149.

104. *Commentary* on Ezekiel 1:1. For a more comprehensive look at Calvin's comprehensive piety, see Joel R. Beeke, *Living for God's Glory: An Introduction to Calvinism* (Orlando, Fla.: Reformation Trust, 2008), 173–88.

105. *Commentary* on John 20:23.

106. Calvin *The Mystery of Godliness*, 122.

free to apply his sermon to those events in practical, experiential, and moralistic ways.[107]

Nevertheless, the ultimate goal of all preaching must be to glorify the triune God. Calvin's preaching, therefore, clearly focused on the Father, Son, and Holy Spirit. Everywhere God is front and center, particularly as the God of salvation. God is exalted and man is abased. Powerful preaching, for Calvin, stresses how heinous sin is and how amazing grace is. Christ is held before us as our Savior who was horribly afflicted for our sins and wonderfully resurrected for us, clothed in the gospel. The gospel is a mirror in which we behold our Mediator, who is the very image of God.[108] The Spirit of God reveals Christ and His salvation to us. The wonder of the gospel moves us to worshipful silence and awe in the presence of the Father, the Son, and the Spirit. Parker summarizes this well:

> The preacher's purpose is directed first of all towards God. He preaches in order that God may be glorified. The very act of declaring the Gospel is a praising and exalting of God in his mighty acts. Every preaching of God's Word is a *Te Deum Laudamus*, a uniting with the heavens and all the powers therein, with the glorious company of the Apostles, the goodly fellowship of the Prophets, the noble army of Martyrs, and the holy Church throughout all the world, in the praise and worship of God. And when the purpose is directed towards man it does not lose its character of praise of God, for it is he who saves, who reforms lives, who cares for and preserves, and therefore is to be thanked, praised, worshipped.[109]

A Quick Summary of Faithful, Powerful Preaching

Calvin's sermons were widely circulated during his lifetime and after his death. While they were powerful and influential, Calvin had weaknesses in preaching, like any other preacher. Even his protégé,

107. A. Mitchell Hunter, "Calvin as a Preacher," *Expository Times*, 30, 12 (Sept 1919): 563.

108. Cf. Zachman, *John Calvin as Teacher, Pastor, and Theologian*, 199–203.

109. Parker, *Calvin's Preaching*, 46.

Theodore Beza, recognized that he lacked certain gifts. Beza said that Calvin, Guillaume Farel, and Pierre Viret all had different styles of preaching: "Farel excelled in a certain sublimity of mind, so that nobody could either hear his thunders without trembling, or listen to his most fervent prayers without feeling as it were carried up into heaven. Viret possessed such winning eloquence, that his entranced audience hung upon his lips. Calvin never spoke without filling the mind of the hearer with the most weighty sentiments. I have often thought a preacher compounded of the three would have been absolutely perfect."[110]

Though every preacher has shortcomings, Calvin offers us a standard by which to measure our own preaching and the preaching around us. Calvin's times were very different from our own, and an attempt to imitate him would be wrong. But the main contours of Calvin's preaching should be followed, no matter what, to maintain genuine Word-based and Spirit-applied preaching today.

Calvin lived to preach. He knew that as the pulpit goes, so goes the church, and ultimately, the nation. His teaching on faithful, powerful preaching was superlative. Let us summarize seven characteristics of powerful preaching, according to Calvin:

First is its focus and dependence on the written Word of God. The Scriptures are both the motivation for and the content of preaching. They are the supreme rule in preaching, for they lend authority to the preached Word and, when preaching is faithful to the Word, it becomes the very Word of God Himself. Any teaching that derives its authority from any other source is not Christian preaching. God has commissioned ambassadors to preach the message of their Master and that alone.

Second is its careful and systematic exegesis. The Word of God set the agenda for Calvin's preaching, and his consecutive exposition of that Word manifested this principle. He was concerned that all preachers be trained and learned in the Word so they could faithfully exegete it.

Third is its simplicity and applicability. Though Calvin demanded that every preacher be a scholar of the Word, he did not require such

110. Theodore Beza, "The Life of John Calvin," in *Selected Works of John Calvin: Tracts and Letters* (Edinburgh: Banner of Truth Trust, 2009), 1:xxxix.

men to show off their learning with complicated and verbose sermons. Rather, he advocated brevity and simplicity. His own preaching also showed that he valued application. A sermon without application was no sermon at all.

Fourth is its dependence on the Spirit. Calvin carefully navigated between two extremes, holding to the right course by distinguishing but *not* separating the Word and the Spirit. The authority of the Word comes from its divine Author, but without the work of the Spirit, the Word will have no effect on listeners. The preacher is thus helpless to change the hearts and lives of listeners, and must proceed in total dependence on the Spirit.

Fifth is its experiential emphasis. Calvin was an experiential theologian and preacher who tried to keep in balance how spiritual matters should go in the Christian life, how they do go, and their end goal. He avoided excesses by confining himself to the limits of Scripture and by tying the Spirit's experiential work to Scripture. At the same time, he used experiential preaching to minister to the needs of believers through large dosages of application and as a discriminatory tool for unbelievers. Above all, the purpose of his experiential emphases was to lead believers to glorify the Trinity through Jesus Christ.

Sixth is its piety, both in the preacher and in listeners. Such piety is necessary in the preacher to produce faithful sermons and—by the grace of the Spirit—to produce piety in those who listen. The great goal of preaching is to bring men and women closer to Christ and to a faithful walk with Him.

Seventh is its focus on union with Christ, the Trinity, and God's glory. All preaching must be done *soli Deo gloria*—to the Father, to the Son, and to the Holy Spirit, "for of him, and through him, and to him, are all things: to whom be glory for ever" (Rom. 11:36). That is the apex of all preaching, for in such preaching, God is exalted and we are rightly humbled before Him in awe and worship.

Calvin could have preached many things from his pulpit in Geneva, but he chose to preach the Word of God. Though we could preach many things from our pulpits, we too must preach nothing but the same timeless Word. If we are not preachers, we must tolerate nothing less than the proclamation of the Scriptures from the preachers we hear.

Calvin believed in preaching. So should we. The church today does not need CEO administrators, public relation manipulators, ivory-tower academicians, or felt-needs ministers. It needs faithful Bible-expounding, Christ-honoring, man-humbling, God-exalting preaching. Only this Word can change the world, as it did in Calvin's time.

Faithful, powerful preaching is not an option. God demands it and gives it; His people need it and relish it; and those of us who are preachers are responsible to pray for it and to provide it. In dependence on the Spirit of God, we must start with our own hearts, daily applying the Word of God to our own lives, so that we know by experience what sinful hearts need to hear. We must know and love our people so that we can address the trials and temptations they encounter. And then, crying to the Spirit of Christ to fill us, we must step into the pulpit, determined to please God by presenting His Word clearly, trusting that when we preach biblically, doctrinally, experientially, and practically, it *will* change the world. The Spirit's power will be unleashed.

A new generation of such preachers is this world's greatest present need. Let us pray daily for it.

Contributors

Dr. Joel R. Beeke is president and professor of systematic theology and homiletics at Puritan Reformed Theological Seminary, a pastor of the Heritage Netherlands Reformed Congregation in Grand Rapids, Michigan, editor of *Banner of Sovereign Grace Truth,* editorial director of Reformation Heritage Books, president of Inheritance Publishers, and vice-president of the Dutch Reformed Translation Society. He has written, co-authored, or edited sixty books (most recently, *Living for God's Glory: An Introduction to Calvinism, Meet the Puritans, Contagious Christian Living, Reformation Heroes, Calvin for Today,* and *Striving Against Satan*), and contributed fifteen hundred articles to Reformed books, journals, periodicals, and encyclopedias. His Ph.D. is in Reformation and Post-Reformation theology from Westminster Theological Seminary. He is frequently called upon to lecture at seminaries and to speak at Reformed conferences around the world. He and his wife, Mary, have three children.

Dr. Sinclair B. Ferguson is the senior pastor of First Presbyterian Church in Columbia, South Carolina, a professor of Systematic Theology at Westminster Seminary in Dallas, Texas, a visiting professor at Puritan Reformed Theological Seminary in Grand Rapids, Michigan, an assistant editor and trustee of the Banner of Truth Trust in Scotland, and an Alliance Council member. He has authored a few dozen books, including *The Holy Spirit, Taking the Christian Life Seriously,* and *Know Your Christian Life.* His M.A. and Ph.D. degrees were awarded by the University of Aberdeen, Scotland. He is frequently called upon to lecture at seminaries and to speak at conferences worldwide. He and his wife, Dorothy, have four children.

Rev. Ian Hamilton is minister of Cambridge Presbyterian Church, England. Prior to this he was minister of Loudoun Church of Scotland, Ayrshire, from 1979–1999. He has written, *The Erosion of Calvinst Orthodoxy* (soon to be re-published by Christian Focus); *The Letters of John,* and *Calvin's Doctrine of Holy Scripture,* along with a number of chapters in *Festschrifts.* He also serves on the boards of the Banner of Truth, Greenville Presbyterian Theological

Seminary, and London Theological Seminary. He and his wife, Joan, have four children.

Dr. Anthony N. S. Lane is Professor of Historical Theology at London School of Theology, where he has taught since 1973. He has written seven books, including *A Concise History of Christian Thought, John Calvin: Student of the Church Fathers, Justification by Faith in Catholic-Protestant Dialogue: An Evangelical Assessment,* and (most recently) *A Reader's Guide to Calvin's Institutes.* He has edited a number of texts including *Calvin's Bondage and Liberation of the Will* (in the Latin original and in English translation) and has edited five other books. He has a D.D. from Oxford University. He and his wife, Maggie, have two grown-up daughters.

Ray Pennings is a Senior Fellow with Cardus, Chair of the Redeemer University Board of Governors, a part-time student at Puritan Reformed Theological Seminary, and a member of the Free Reformed Church of Calgary, Alberta. He and his wife have one child.

Dr. Paul Wells is dean at the Reformed Seminary in Aix-en-Provence, France, where he has taught Systematic Theology since 1972. He studied at Liverpool University in England (B.A., M.A.) and Westminster Theological Seminary in Philadelphia (M.Div., 1972). His doctoral thesis at the Free University of Amsterdam, *James Barr and the Bible: Critique of a New Liberalism,* was published in 1980 (Presbyterian and Reformed). Works in French include books on the doctrine of Scripture, the words of Christ from the cross, the Christian life, commentaries on the Lord's Prayer and the Apostles' Creed, and an introduction to the Christian faith for students. *Cross Words* (Christian Focus, 2006), has also been published in French and Dutch. He published a new translation and edition of Calvin's *Institutes* in modern French in 2009. He has been editor of *La Revue réformée*, a leading evangelical journal in French, since 1982.

Dr. Garry J. Williams is Director of the John Owen Centre at London Theological Seminary in England and Visiting Professor of Historical Theology at Westminster Theological Seminary, Philadelphia. His academic publications have focused on the origins of evangelicalism and on penal substitutionary atonement. His D.Phil. from the University of Oxford was on Hugo Grotius's doctrine of the atonement. He is married to Fiona and they have four young children.